ULTIMATE BIBLE TRIVIA

Fun-Filled Facts & Trivia Questions to
Find Out How Much You Really Know!

By
ANN SISON

Copyright 2021. Ann Sison.

Bridge Press.

bp@purplelink.org

All Rights Reserved.

No part of this book may be reproduced or transmitted in any form or by any means, electronic or mechanical, including photocopying, recording, or by any other form without written permission from the publisher.

ISBN: 978-1-955149-10-5

Please consider writing a review!

Just visit: purplelink.org/review

TABLE OF CONTENTS:

Introduction 1

THE OLD TESTAMENT 3

CHAPTER 1: The Torah 4
Trivia Time! 4
Answers 9
Did You Know? 11

CHAPTER 2: The Historical Books 15
Trivia Time! 15
Answers 20
Did You Know? 22

CHAPTER 3: Poetry Books 26
Trivia Time! 26
Answers 31
Did You Know? 33

CHAPTER 4: Wisdom Books 35
Trivia Time! 35

Answers..40
Did You Know?..42

CHAPTER 5: THE PROPHETS.................................44
Trivia Time!..44
Answers..49
Did You Know?..51

THE NEW TESTAMENT............................ 55

CHAPTER 6: THE GOSPELS...................................56
Trivia Time!..56
Answers..61
Did You Know?..63

CHAPTER 7: ACTS...67
Trivia Time!..67
Answers..71
Did You Know?..73

CHAPTER 8: PAUL'S EPISTLES................................77
Trivia Time!..77
Answers..82
Did You Know?..84

CHAPTER 9: OTHER LETTERS..................................86
   Trivia Time!..86
   Answers..91
   Did You Know?...93

CHAPTER 10: REVELATION 95
   Trivia Time!..95
   Answers..100
   Did You Know?...102

ABOUT THE BIBLE.................................. 105

CHAPTER 11: WOMEN IN THE BIBLE 106
   Trivia Time!..106
   Answers..111
   Did You Know?...113

CHAPTER 12: BIBLE HEROES 117
   Trivia Time!..117
   Answers..122
   Did You Know?...124

CHAPTER 13: MIRACLES OF JESUS 127
   Trivia Time!..127
   Answers..132

Did You Know? 134

CHAPTER 14: PARABLES OF JESUS 137
    Trivia Time! 137
    Answers 142
    Did You Know? 144

CHAPTER 15: BIBLICAL HISTORY &
ARCHEOLOGY 147
    Trivia Time! 147
    Answers 152
    Did You Know? 154

INTRODUCTION

As the most read book of all time, the Bible has been read for many centuries and translated into more than seven hundred languages. In the last fifty years alone, nearly four billion copies of the Bible were printed and treasured by households all over the world.

Whether you wish to check your Biblical literacy or want a fun crash course in popular stories from the Bible, this book is for you! Many families have invested hours studying favorite Bible stories like Noah's Ark, Moses and the Exodus, David and Goliath, and Jesus Walking on Water. This book includes trivia on those as well as dives into the lesser-known topics like the exploits of the judges of Israel and the words of the minor prophets.

This trivia book covers both the history and the content of the Bible, beginning with Genesis and covering additional topics like Bible heroes and women of the Bible. A series of multiple-choice and true-or-false questions open each chapter, with the corresponding answers in the next section. A bonus "Did You Know?" feature chock-full of interesting facts and stories are found at the end of each chapter to deepen your Biblical knowledge.

The facts and tidbits in this trivia book were designed to cover a variety of topics and stories, with questions that are appropriate for all ages and all levels of Biblical knowledge.

Think you might be a Bible expert? Test your Bible knowledge with these fun and informative trivia questions and find out how much you truly know!

So, grab your favorite scriptures, and let's get started!

THE OLD TESTAMENT

CHAPTER 1:
THE TORAH

TRIVIA TIME!

1. How many mothers gave birth to the twelve sons of Jacob?
    a. One
    b. Two
    c. Three
    d. Four

2. Who is said to have written the first five books of the Bible (Genesis, Exodus, Leviticus, Numbers, and Deuteronomy?)
    a. Noah
    b. Shem
    c. Moses
    d. Abraham

3. True or false: Moses ascended to meet with God on Mount Sinai more than once.

4. True or false: When Jacob and Esau were born, Jacob was born first.

5. Which of Joseph's brothers devised the plan to sell him into slavery rather than kill him?
   a. Judah
   b. Reuben
   c. Simeon
   d. Benjamin

6. Which of these were not one of the original twelve sons/tribes of Israel?
   a. Dan
   b. Levi
   c. Manasseh
   d. Issachar

7. True or false: The first bird that Noah sent out from the Ark after the flood was a raven.

8. Moses sought refuge in the desert of Midian for this many years after fleeing Egypt for killing an Egyptian:
   a. Seven
   b. Ten
   c. Fourteen
   d. Forty

9. True or false: The ten plagues of Egypt each lasted for seven days and nights.

10. Why was Joseph thrown into prison while in Egypt?
    a. His brothers put him there
    b. He disobeyed the Pharaoh

c. He was accused of abusing his master's wife
   d. He tried to kill his master's wife

11. What did God tell Moses to remove at the burning bush?
    a. His sandals
    b. His staff
    c. His cloak
    d. His head covering

12. What did Rebekah do upon seeing Isaac, who was about to become her husband?
    a. Hid in the servant's luggage
    b. Quickly got off her camel to greet him
    c. Cried tears of joy for her marriage
    d. Put on her bridal garments

13. Abraham journeyed to the promised land from the land of ____.
    a. Timnah
    b. Ur
    c. Babel
    d. Canaan

14. Which of the following is NOT one of the ten plagues that befell Egypt?
    a. Flies
    b. Lice
    c. Flood
    d. Turning the Nile River to blood

15. Which wife was buried with Jacob in the "Cave of the Patriarchs?"
    a. Rachel
    b. Leah
    c. Bilhah
    d. Zilpah

16. Who told Abraham to send Hagar and her son away after the birth of Isaac?
    a. Isaac
    b. God
    c. Sarah
    d. Three messengers

17. Which of these is not one of the ten commandments?
    a. Love your neighbor
    b. Honor your father and mother
    c. Do not take the Lord's name in vain
    d. Honor the Sabbath day and keep it holy

18. How many years did it take for Jacob to reunite with his brother Esau?
    a. Seven years
    b. Fourteen years
    c. Twenty years
    d. Never

19. The Israelites complained about all of the following in the wilderness, except:

    a. Lack of food
    b. Lack of water
    c. The long walk
    d. Moses and the other leaders
20. True or false: After Adam and Eve were kicked out of the Garden of Eden, the gate to the Garden was guarded by special angels with a sword.

ANSWERS

1. D – Four (Genesis 35: 23-26)

2. C – Moses; although not specifically stated, there are many references to the Laws of Moses in Joshua, Kings 1, and Kings 2, and the Talmud attributes the first five books to Moses (Joshua 1: 7-8; 8:32, 34, 22:5; Kings 2:3; 2 Kings 14:6; 21:8; Ezra 6:18).

3. True; Moses met with God on the mountain at least twice and possibly as many as seven times (Exodus 19, Exodus 34:29).

4. False; Esau was born first with Jacob holding on to his foot (Genesis 25: 19-26).

5. A – Judah (Genesis 37)

6. C – Manasseh (Deuteronomy 27: 12-13)

7. True; the dove was sent later (Genesis 8: 6-7).

8. D – Forty (Acts 7: 30-54)

9. False; the truth is that nobody knows as it was not specified in the Bible. Scholars have come to many conclusions over the years, coming to the conclusion that the plagues lasted collectively anywhere from a month to a full year (as stated in the Jewish Mishnah). Information on the plagues of Egypt is found in Exodus.

10. C – His master's wife accused him of harming her (Genesis 39: 19-21).

11. A – His sandals (Exodus 3:5)

12. B – She quickly got off her camel to greet him (Genesis 24: 64).

13. B – Ur (Genesis 15:7)

14. C – Flood (Exodus 7:11)

15. B – Leah (Genesis 49:29-31)

16. C – Sarah (Genesis 21:9)

17. A – Love your neighbor (Exodus 20:3-20:17)

18. C – Twenty years (Genesis 31:3, 32:10)

19. C – The long walk (Exodus 15-17)

20. True; it was guarded by cherubim, later symbolized in the Ark of the Covenant (Genesis 3:24).

DID YOU KNOW?

- The Torah is comprised of the first five books of the Bible: Genesis, Exodus, Leviticus, Numbers, and Deuteronomy. Tradition holds that it was written by Moses sometime during the 14th century BC. However, some scholars think that the Torah in the form we have today was compiled in the sixth century BC during the Babylonian exile.

- The word Genesis comes from a Greek word for "beginning." The book of Genesis begins with the creation of the world and includes a great amount of historical narrative, up until the time of Joseph's death in Egypt.

- Genesis covers the longest time period of any book in the Bible, detailing the history of a time span of more than 2,000 years.

- The name Exodus comes from a Greek word meaning "the road out," and the book details the departure of the Israelites from Egypt, their wanderings in the desert, and the creation of the tabernacle.

- The book of Leviticus was written as a set of instructions for the Levites and specifically the priests. In this book, we find various rules about worship, purity, and sacrifices.

- The book of Numbers was given its name because of the two "numberings" (or censuses) of the people that took place in this book. In Hebrew, the name is "Bmidbar," which means "in the wilderness." This book details the account of the wanderings in the desert for an entire generation until the time of the conquest.

- The meaning of the name Deuteronomy is "second law" or "repeated law." The book of Deuteronomy is a compilation of Moses's final words to the people of Israel as he repeated the instructions of the law to the new generation of Israelites. These three sermons expand upon what was given on Mt. Sinai. The book concludes with the death of Moses on Mount Nebo.

- In the book of Leviticus, instructions for infant circumcision say that the procedure must not be performed until the eighth day. Later scientific research has shown that newborn levels of Vitamin K are highest on this day, which is important because Vitamin K plays a role in blood clotting that is vital after such a surgery.

- The book of Leviticus outlines seven Holy days the Israelites were to observe each year. These days are The Passover, The Feast of Unleavened Bread, The Feast of First Fruits, The Feast of Weeks, The Feast of Trumpets, The Day of Atonement, and The Feast of Tabernacles.

- God often acts on one of these seven Holy days from Leviticus. For example, the giving of the Torah at Mount Sinai and the giving of the Holy Spirit at the upper room in Acts both happened on the same Jewish Holy day – Shavuot (what you may know as Pentecost or the Feast of Weeks).

- You might not believe it, but Noah's Ark housed more than just two of every animal. In fact, Noah was instructed in Genesis 7 to bring seven pairs of all clean animals onboard the Ark and two of each unclean animal. This is because the clean animals were sacrificed later and potentially used for food.

- In the story of Jacob and Esau, Jewish tradition attests that Rachel and Leah might have also been twins, originally intended for one to marry each brother. However, Esau went against his parent's wishes to marry within the faith and instead married a Canaanite woman. Therefore, Jacob received both wives at the hand of Laban's deceit.

- During their years of wandering in the wilderness, the Israelites were instructed to camp around the tabernacle in a certain pattern. The camp of Ephraim was located on the West side of the tabernacle and consisted of the tribes of Benjamin (35,400 people), Manasseh (32,200 people), and Ephraim (40,500 people). The camp of Dan was located on the North side and included the tribes of Dan (62,700 people),

Asher (41,500 people), and Naphtali (53,400 people). The camp of Judah was located on the East side and held the tribes of Judah (74,600 people), Issachar (54,400 people), and Zebulun (57,400 people). The camp of Reuben completed the concentric layout to the South and consisted of the tribes of Gad (45,650 people), Simeon (59,300 people), and Reuben (46,500 people). In the center, the tribe of Levi was joined with the clans of Gershon, Merari, and Kohath with Moses, Aaron, and Moses's two living sons in front of the tent.

- The lesser-known story of Moses lifting up a snake on his staff to heal the people who had been bitten by venomous snakes in the wilderness has a parallel in the New Testament. As John noted in John 3:14-15, just "as Moses lifted up the serpent in the wilderness, so must the Son of Man be lifted up that whoever believes in Him may have eternal life."

CHAPTER 2:
THE HISTORICAL BOOKS

TRIVIA TIME!

1. Why did Samuel grow up at the tabernacle in service to the Lord?
    a. He was an orphan.
    b. His mother made a vow before he was born.
    c. His father was the High Priest.
    d. He ran away from home.

2. Who was the first judge to rule over Israel?
    a. Othniel
    b. Deborah
    c. Gideon
    d. Joshua

3. Who was the prophet that rebuked King David for his sin against Bathsheba?
    a. Jeremiah
    b. Isaiah
    c. Absalom
    d. Nathan

4. Where was the first temple built by King Solomon?
    a. In the city of Shiloh
    b. On the Mount of Olives
    c. Mount Moriah
    d. In the Valley of Hinnom

5. What was the name of the original Queen in the book of Esther?
    a. Hadassah
    b. Vashti
    c. Sheba
    d. Jezebel

6. True or false: Ruth knew that the field where she began working belonged to Naomi's relative Boaz.

7. What Canaanite city did the Israelites burn with fire after the war at Jericho?
    a. Gibeon
    b. Ai
    c. Jerusalem
    d. Hebron

8. True or false: Elisha was the first prophet to perform the miracle of resurrection.

9. True or false: Saul was anointed the first King of Israel when he went looking for his father's donkeys.

10. Which of these women was not a wife of King David?
    a. Bathsheba
    b. Abigail

c. Michal
   d. Naamah

11. Which king tried to summon the prophet Samuel from beyond the grave?
    a. King Solomon
    b. King Saul
    c. King David
    d. King Ahab

12. True or false: When the Philistines stole the Ark of the Covenant, their statue of the false god Dagon was found bowing down to it.

13. True or false: David had a chance to kill King Saul, and he didn't take it.

14. Obed, the son of Ruth and Boaz, was the father of whom?
    a. King Saul
    b. King David
    c. Jesse
    d. Joseph

15. How did the Israelites react to the construction of the second temple?
    a. They wept
    b. They were afraid
    c. They were angry
    d. They made a great feast

16. What did King Saul do when his name was drawn by lots to become King?
    a. Praised and thanked God
    b. Demanded the crowd bow to him
    c. Ran away
    d. Hid among the luggage

17. Gideon was famous for which of these things?
    a. Asking for a sign from God
    b. Running away from a battle
    c. Prophesying victory over Israel's enemies
    d. Growing out his long hair

18. The queen of what country came to see King Solomon?
    a. Babylon
    b. Sheba
    c. Egypt
    d. Persia

19. Which of these was not something that King Solomon did?
    a. Built the first temple in Jerusalem
    b. Asked God for wisdom above any other thing
    c. Ordered the killing of the firstborn in order to display his power
    d. Turned away to false idols at the end of his life

20. What happened after the seventh time the Israelites marched around Jericho?

a. The walls fell down
b. The city caught on fire
c. Rahab rescued the Israelites
d. The people of the city ran away

ANSWERS

1. B – His mother made a vow before he was born (1 Samuel 1:11).

2. A – Othniel (Judges 3:7-11)

3. D – Nathan (Samuel 2:12)

4. C – Mount Moriah (2 Chronicles 3:1)

5. B – Vashti (Esther 1:11)

6. False; the book of Ruth records that she "just so happened" to glean there (Ruth 2).

7. B – Ai (Joshua 8:1-28)

8. False; Elijah first raised the widow of Zarephath's son from the dead (1 Kings 17:7-16.).

9. True; King Saul was looking for his father's lost donkeys when he went to visit Samuel the seer (1 Samuel 9:3).

10. D – Naamah (2 Samuel 3: 13-15, 1 Samuel 25, 2 Samuel 11)

11. B – King Saul (1 Samuel 28:15)

12. True; it happened twice, and on the second time, the head and hands of Dagon were cut off as well (1 Samuel 5:2-5).

13. True; when he was hiding in the cave, David was close enough to King Saul to cut a corner of his robe. He used this as evidence to prove to Saul he would not harm him while he was King (1 Samuel 24).

14. C – Jesse (the father of King David) (Ruth 4:22)

15. A – They wept (Ezra 3:10-13).

16. D – He hid among the luggage (1 Samuel 10:20).

17. A – Asking for a sign from God (Judges 6:33)

18. B – Sheba (1 Kings 10: 1-13)

19. C – Ordered the killing of the firstborn in order to display his power (1 Kings 6, 1 Kings 3:1-15, 1 Kings 11)

20. A – The walls fell down (Joshua 6:1-27).

DID YOU KNOW?

- There are twelve books that are commonly referred to as the historical books of the Old Testament. These books are Joshua, Judges, Ruth, 1 Samuel, 2 Samuel, 1 Kings, 2 Kings, 1 Chronicles, 2 Chronicles, Ezra, Nehemiah, and Esther.

- These twelve historical books cover a time period of almost 1,000 years, from the conquest of the land until the return from the Babylonian exile.

- In addition, Catholic and Orthodox Bibles contain Tobit, Judith, and Maccabees.

- The book of Joshua is titled in honor of Israel's second leader, whose name appropriately meant "salvation."

- Many Bible scholars think that Caleb (who, together with Joshua, sent back a "good report" from the Promised Land) was biologically a Gentile who became a part of the tribe of Judah. Caleb is listed in Numbers 32:12 as the son of Jephunneh the Kenizzite, making his lineage that of a Canaanite. If this is indeed true, then as he joins together with Joshua, we see Jew and Gentile working together to fulfill the promises of God.

- Originally, Israel was ruled by judges and not kings. These judges decided between the people, heard from God, and sometimes delivered the nation from war. The book of Judges details the three and a half centuries between Joshua's death and the beginning of Israel's kings' period with King Saul in 1020 BC.

- The period of kings did not last long, at least not as a united nation. The Kingdom of Israel was divided into two kingdoms after the reign of King Solomon.

- The Northern Kingdom of Israel was made up of ten tribes, and the Southern Kingdom of Judah was made up of two tribes. Of all the kings who ruled over the kingdoms, very few were recorded as being righteous kings.

- In the original Hebrew Bible, 1 & 2 Chronicles were together as one book, as were 1 & 2 Kings and 1 & 2 Samuel. They were later split to make them easier to read.

- Throughout all of the historical books, contextual references are often made to many real people and places that can be verified today. These references don't just include things local to Israel but also foreign rulers, wars, and cities. For example, there was King Sennacherib of Assyria, who sieged but failed to capture Jerusalem—events corroborated by the archeological discovery of Sennacherib's prism.

- The books of 1 & 2 Kings and 1 & 2 Chronicles are often very similar and detail many of the same events. So why have two different records? Kings focus more on the historical events in chronological order while trying to give a parallel narrative of both the Northern and the Southern Kingdoms. On the other hand, Chronicles is more concerned with the spiritual aspects of the time period and focuses mostly on the Southern Kingdom of Judah.

- The title given to the books of Chronicles by the Septuagint (an early Greek translation of the scriptures) is "paralipomena," which roughly means "things left out." This gives us a clue of why the book was compiled, most likely by Ezra, at the return of the Israelites from exile.

- There were a few phases to the return from exile. King Cyrus issued a decree to allow the Jews to return, and King Darius later made sure it was carried out. The first return to rebuild was led by Zerubbabel, and the second was led by Ezra.

- Not all of the people who were residing in exile chose to return at the end of the exile period. Even as the city of Jerusalem and its temple were rebuilt, only a small percentage came back to the land of Israel. Out of more than two million people, only around 50,000 made the journey back home.

- As the people of Israel came back to the land, Ezra and Nehemiah were the two important leaders detailed in scripture. Ezra was a priest and scribe credited with the religious restoration of Israel, while

Nehemiah was known for rebuilding the city walls and contributing to the physical restoration of Jerusalem.

- Scripture says that those who witnessed the beauty and glory of the first temple were overcome with emotion at the laying of the foundation of the second. In one of the most poignant verses in all of scripture, Ezra 3:13 details how the cry of the elders was drowned out by the joyful shouting of the people.

- Ezra, the Jewish priest and scribe who reintroduced the Torah to the people after the return from Babylonian exile, may have written more than just the book of Ezra. The books of 1 and 2 Chronicles are also most commonly attributed to his authorship. In addition, Jewish tradition holds that Ezra and the prophet Malachi may have been one and the same man.

- There are also some Apocryphal writings attributed to Ezra known as 1 and 2 Esdras that were contained in the original *1611 King James Bible* and still appear in some Catholic, Episcopal, Ethiopian, and Greek Orthodox canons today.

CHAPTER 3:
POETRY BOOKS

TRIVIA TIME!

1. Psalm 119 is an acrostic poem dedicated to which concept?
    a. God's love
    b. God's law
    c. God's righteousness
    d. God's wrath

2. What comes next in this iconic Psalm "He makes me lie down in green pastures?"
    a. He anoints my head with oil.
    b. He sets a table before me in the presence of my enemies.
    c. He leads me beside still waters.
    d. He leads me in paths of righteousness for His name's sake.

3. What does the word "Selah" mean?
    a. Pause
    b. Sing

c. Praise Him
   d. Pray
4. In Song of Solomon, the writer compares his lover's neck to:
   a. A gazelle
   b. A vine
   c. The Tower of David
   d. A fountain
5. Complete this line from Song of Solomon: "Your love is better than ___."
   a. The morning sun
   b. Rubies
   c. Pearls
   d. Wine
6. True or false: Solomon wrote a few Psalms of his own.
7. Finish this famous Psalm: "Your word is a lamp unto my feet ___."
   a. And a light unto my path
   b. And you have set my feet on a rock
   c. Your word is my sword and shield
   d. Though I walk through the valley of the shadow of death, I will fear no evil
8. Which of these song lyrics is not a line from the Psalms?
   a. "Whom shall I fear?"
   b. "Deep cries out to deep"

c. "I will sing of Your love forever"
  d. "Blessed be the name of the Lord…You give and take away"

9. In Psalm 27:1, David refers to the Lord as his light and his ___:
   a. Shield
   b. Lamp
   c. Sword
   d. Salvation

10. In Psalm 18, David wrote, "He makes my feet like ___."
    a. A deer
    b. A rock
    c. A mountain
    d. A lion

11. Which of these Psalms is often read as a prayer for protection?
    a. Psalm 119
    b. Psalm 91
    c. Psalm 40
    d. Psalm 21

12. True or false: The Psalms are the only place in the Bible where songs are found.

13. Fill in the blank of this famous line in Psalm 42: "As a ___ pants for flowing streams, so pants my soul for you, O God."

a. Dog
   b. Deer
   c. Goat
   d. Sheep

14. True or false: There is a Psalm attributed to Moses.

15. Who is the most likely author of the book of Lamentations?
    a. Jeremiah
    b. Daniel
    c. David
    d. Solomon

16. The theme of the book of Lamentations is:
    a. Advice for wise living
    b. Life is meaningless without God
    c. Mourning over sin and the destruction of Jerusalem
    d. Sorrow between star-crossed lovers

17. Complete this famous Psalm: "This is the day that the LORD has made; let us __."
    a. Sing praises to the Most High God
    b. Rejoice and be glad in it
    c. Pray to the Most High God
    d. Come before his throne with joy

18. What is the missing word in this line from Psalm 95? "Let us come into His presence with _____; let us make a joyful noise to him with songs of praise!"

a. Shouting
   b. Laughter
   c. Joy
   d. Thanksgiving

19. Psalm 34:8 states: "Oh, ___ and see that the LORD is good!"
    a. Pray
    b. Look
    c. Taste
    d. Hear

20. True or false: The book of Lamentations is the only book that does not include the promise of future hope in God's restoration of His people.

ANSWERS

1. B - God's law (Psalm 119)
2. C - He leads me beside still waters (Psalm 23:2)
3. A - Pause
4. C - The Tower of David (Solomon 4:4)
5. D - Wine (Song of Solomon 4:10)
6. True; at least two Psalms and possibly others are attributed to King Solomon (Psalm 72, possibly Psalm 17 and 18).
7. A - And a light unto my path (Psalm 119:105)
8. D - "Blessed be the name of the Lord...You give and take away" (Psalm 21, 42:7, Psalm 89).
9. D - Salvation (Psalm 27:1)
10. A - A deer (Psalm 18)
11. B - Psalm 91
12. False; there are many other places in the Bible where songs are recorded (like "The Song of Moses" in Exodus 15).
13. B - Deer (Psalm 42)
14. True; Moses is said to have written Psalm 90 - "A prayer of Moses" (Psalm 90)."

15. A – Jeremiah

16. C – Mourning over sin and the destruction of Jerusalem

17. B – Rejoice and be glad in it (Psalm 118:4)

18. D – Thanksgiving (Psalm 95)

19. C – Taste (Psalm 34:8)

20. False; like many other Biblical books, Lamentations also includes a hopeful message for the future (Lamentation 3:21-33).

DID YOU KNOW?

- There are 150 different Psalms written over a period of approximately 1,000 years from Moses to Solomon.

- Only about half of the Psalms were actually written by King David. Others were written by musical families, such as the sons of Korah, and some are anonymous. Most modern Bibles record the author at the beginning of each Psalm.

- The word "psalm" comes from the Greek word "psalmos" which means "song sung to a harp."

- There are dozens of Messianic prophecies scattered throughout the Psalms. Scholars see at least seventy with clear references to the Messiah and potentially many more. Many of these prophecies from the Psalms are quoted by the various New Testament writers and even Jesus Himself. For example, on the cross, when Jesus cries out, "My God, my God, why hast thou forsaken me?" he was referencing the opening verse of Psalm 22.

- The book of Psalms has 150 chapters, making it the lengthiest book of the Bible in terms of chapters. It is more than 30,000 words long (in the original language), making it the third wordiest book of the Bible, after Jeremiah and Genesis.

- A collection of Psalms known as the Psalms of Ascent were sung by pilgrims ascending to the temple in Jerusalem. This beautiful section of scripture extends from Psalm 120 to Psalm 134 and includes themes of joy, rest, and thanksgiving.

- Psalms 113-118, as well as Psalm 136, are commonly read at the festival of Passover. In fact, Jesus Himself might have recited or sang these Psalms with His disciples at the Last Supper. Matthew 26:30 records Jesus and His disciples singing a hymn.

- The Song of Solomon (also called the "Song of Songs") was a love song written by King Solomon, perhaps to his bride (a Shulamite girl), but most scholars agree that it also parallels God's love for Israel.

- The book of Lamentations is traditionally read on the Jewish holiday of Tisha B'Av to commemorate and mourn the destruction of the Jewish temple.

- The book of Lamentations is also known as "The Book of Tears."

CHAPTER 4:
WISDOM BOOKS

TRIVIA TIME!

1. The first nine chapters of Proverbs focus heavily on which sin?

    a. Greed
    b. Pride
    c. Lust
    d. Adultery

2. In the chapters of Proverbs, wisdom is personified as a ____.

    a. Lion
    b. Woman
    c. Teacher
    d. Master

3. In Proverbs 27, a nagging wife is famously compared to what?

    a. A constant dripping
    b. A thorn in the side of her husband

    c. Cancer in the bones
    d. A poisonous tongue
4. In Proverbs 7:27, the author warns that the adulterous woman's house leads to:
    a. Ruin
    b. Sheol
    c. Destruction
    d. Poverty
5. Complete this Proverb: "___ is the beginning of wisdom."
    a. Fear of the Lord
    b. Love
    c. Knowledge
    d. Pride
6. Proverbs 3:5 reads: "Trust in the LORD with all your heart and lean not on ____."
    a. Yourself
    b. Your feelings
    c. Your emotions
    d. Your own understanding
7. Which of the following verses does NOT come from the book of Proverbs?
    a. "There is a way that appears to be right, but in the end, it leads to death."
    b. "Blessed is the man who walks not in the counsel of the wicked."

    c. "The heart of man plans his way, but the LORD establishes his steps."

    d. "Gracious words are like a honeycomb, sweetness to the soul and health to the body."

8. According to Proverbs 4:23, everything you do flows from this:

    a. God
    b. Your thoughts
    c. Your words
    d. Your heart

9. What is the meaning of "as iron sharpens iron?"

    a. So one man sharpens another
    b. Wisdom keeps a man sharp
    c. Three are better than one
    d. Working hard is the cure for laziness

10. "A cheerful heart is good medicine, but a crushed spirit ____."

    a. Is like cancer in the bones
    b. Dries up the soul
    c. Withers away
    d. Leads to death

11. According to Proverbs 15, what turns away wrath?

    a. A gentle answer
    b. A harsh word
    c. Fear of God
    d. Words as sweet as honey

12. In Proverbs 6:16, there are "six things that the Lord hates, seven that are an abomination to Him." Which of these is not on that list?

    a. Haughty eyes
    b. A lying tongue
    c. A false witness
    d. A lazy sluggard

13. Proverbs 30 mentions four small animals who are very wise. Which is not included?

    a. The ant
    b. The spider
    c. The lizard
    d. The locust

14. According to Proverbs 6:6, the sluggard should consider the ways of what?

    a. God
    b. The righteous
    c. The angels
    d. The ant

15. Proverbs 21:1 informs us that: "The king's heart _____."

    a. Is wicked in all of its ways
    b. Goes wherever the wind blows it
    c. Is a stream of water in the hand of the Lord
    d. Was hardened against the Lord

16. The theme of the book of Ecclesiastes is:
    a. Life is a gift
    b. Life is meaningless without God
    c. Life is meant for having fun
    d. Life is difficult

17. Solomon writes that "for everything, there is a season." Which of these is NOT listed in the famous passage in Ecclesiastes 3?
    a. A time to weep
    b. A time to dance
    c. A time to wed
    d. A time to heal

18. What does Ecclesiastes call a "vanity of vanities?"
    a. Life
    b. Love
    c. Pride
    d. Everything

19. True or false: All of Job's friends blamed Job for his troubles.

20. Who advised Job that he should "curse God and die?"
    a. Satan
    b. His friends
    c. His wife
    d. An angel

ANSWERS

1. D – Adultery (Proverbs 1-9)
2. B – Woman (Proverbs 9: 2,5)
3. A – A constant dripping (Proverbs 7)
4. B – Sheol (Proverbs 7:27)
5. A – Fear of the Lord (Proverbs 9:10)
6. D – Your own understanding (Proverbs 3:15)
7. B – "Blessed is the man who walks not in the counsel of the wicked (Proverbs 14:12, Proverbs 16:9, Proverbs 16:24)."
8. D – Your heart (Proverbs 4:23)
9. A – So one man sharpens another (Proverbs 27:17)
10. B – Dries up the bones (Proverbs 17:22)
11. A – A gentle answer (Proverbs 15)
12. D – A lazy sluggard (Proverbs 16:16)
13. B – The spider (Proverbs 30)
14. D – The ant (Proverbs 6:6)
15. C – Is a stream of water in the hand of the Lord (Proverbs 21:1)
16. B – Life is meaningless without God.
17. C – A time to wed (Ecclesiastes 3:3-4)

18. D – Everything (Ecclesiastes 1:2-11)
19. False; A fourth friend named Elihu arrives later and does not rebuke Job as the others did (Job 32-27).
20. C – His wife (Job 2:9)

DID YOU KNOW?

- Solomon, known as the wisest man who ever lived, is credited with writing the majority of the Proverbs. A few other writers contributed, and an editor likely compiled the writings together at some point to create the book we have today.

- King Solomon may have spoken or recorded more proverbs by King Solomon that we no longer have today. This is because according to 1 Kings 4:32, Solomon "spoke 3,000 proverbs, and his songs were 1,005," but we only have roughly eight hundred sayings preserved for us in the book of Proverbs.

- Psalm 119 is not the only famous acrostic in the Bible! There are many acrostic pieces in the Bible, including Proverbs 31, which is a collection of verses starting with each letter of the Hebrew alphabet.

- The author of the famous Proverbs 31 is written as King Lemuel, a title that many scholars speculate was actually referencing King Solomon. Based on this, many believe that the account of a "Proverbs 31 woman" was inspired by Solomon's mother, Bathsheba, or perhaps from family stories about his ancestress Ruth.

- According to Jewish tradition, Solomon wrote the Song of Solomon in his youth, the various Proverbs throughout his middle life, and the book of Ecclesiastes in his later years.

- The meaning of the word Ecclesiastes comes from the Greek translation of a Hebrew word for preacher and means roughly, "one who speaks to an assembly."

- The author and the exact time that the book of Job was written are both unknown. Many speculate that Job may be the earliest recorded book in the Bible. The story of Job takes place during the time of the Patriarchs.

- According to the Septuagint (a Greek translation of the Old Testament), Job was actually an Edomite king known as King Jobab, possibly the same Jobab mentioned in Genesis 36:33 and 1 Chronicles 1:45.

- King Solomon's wisdom was a result of his prayer to God, asking that He grant him the ability to rule wisely. In fact, because God was pleased that he asked for this above all else, God also granted him what he did not ask for—namely, riches and honor (1 Kings 3).

- Ultimately, King Solomon's riches and honor also led to his downfall as he started to stray spiritually in his later years due to his many wives.

CHAPTER 5:
THE PROPHETS

TRIVIA TIME!

1. The prophet Elisha told Naaman to do what to cure his leprosy?
    a. Pray and fast for three days
    b. Offer sacrifices at the temple in Jerusalem
    c. Go and ask the King
    d. Go and wash himself seven times in the Jordan River

2. The prophet Elijah defeated the prophets of Baal at Mount ____.
    a. Precipice
    b. Carmel
    c. Tabor
    d. Hermon

3. What were the real (Hebrew) names of Shadrach, Meshach, and Abednego?
    a. Michal, Elisha, and Jonah
    b. Daniel, Samuel, and Penuel

    c. Hananiah, Mishael, and Azariah
    d. Shadiel, Meshael, and Abednuel

4. Where did Jonah try to flee instead of delivering God's message to the Ninevites?
    a. Caesarea
    b. Jerusalem
    c. Tarshish
    d. Damascus

5. How long was Daniel in the lion's den?
    a. Three days
    b. One day
    c. One night
    d. Seven hours

6. Which prophet saw the vision of the Valley of Dry Bones?
    a. Elisha
    b. Elijah
    c. Jeremiah
    d. Ezekiel

7. This prophet called himself a "man of unclean lips":
    a. Jeremiah
    b. Isaiah
    c. Ezekiel
    d. Daniel

8. True or false: For three weeks, Daniel refused to eat anything at all in the palace.

9. What did God tell Hosea to do when his wife committed adultery?
    a. Stone her
    b. Divorce her
    c. Love her
    d. Punish her

10. How many times a day would Daniel pray facing Jerusalem?
    a. Three
    b. Five
    c. Seven
    d. Ten

11. This prophet was told to lay on his side for 430 days to prophesy the destruction of Israel and Judah.
    a. Jeremiah
    b. Isaiah
    c. Ezekiel
    d. Micah

12. Which King issued the decree that landed Daniel in the lion's den?
    a. King Nebuchadnezzar
    b. King Darius
    c. King Cyrus
    d. King Xerxes

13. True or false: The Southern Kingdom of Judah fell into exile first.

14. At the *end* of the book of Jonah, the prophet was upset because:
    a. He didn't want to go to Nineveh
    b. His father was killed
    c. He was eaten by the giant fish
    d. A tree he was using for shade withered up

15. This prophet was the last book in the Biblical Old Testament canon:
    a. Hosea
    b. Haggai
    c. Malachi
    d. Micah

16. Jeremiah was also called ____.
    a. The weeping prophet
    b. The hammer
    c. Son of thunder
    d. The faithful prophet

17. The prophecy that the Messiah would be born in Bethlehem comes from:
    a. Ezekiel
    b. Jonah
    c. Jeremiah
    d. Micah

18. According to Joel 2, this comes upon the people during the Day of the Lord:
    a. Ten plagues
    b. A great army
    c. A night as bright as the day
    d. Cannons

19. This prophet was also a judge over Israel:
    a. Jeremiah
    b. Isaiah
    c. Samuel
    d. Samson

20. True or false: There were only prophets in the Old Testament.

ANSWERS

1. D – Go and wash himself seven times in the Jordan River (2 Kings 5:10)

2. B – Carmel (1 Kings 18:16-45)

3. C – Hananiah, Mishael, and Azariah (Daniel 1:7)

4. C – Tarshish (Jonah 1)

5. C – One night (Daniel 6:19)

6. D – Ezekiel (Ezekiel 37)

7. B – Isaiah (Isaiah 6:5)

8. False; Daniel fasted for ten days eating just vegetables and water instead of the king's food and wine (Daniel 1:12).

9. C – Love her (Hosea 3:1)

10. A – Three (Daniel 6:10)

11. C – Ezekiel (Ezekiel 4:4)

12. B – King Darius (Daniel 6:6)

13. False; the Northern Kingdom of Israel was conquered and sent into exile first (1 Chronicles 5:26).

14. D – A tree he was using for shade had withered up (Jonah 4:7-9)

15. C – Malachi

16. A – The weeping prophet (Jeremiah 15)

17. D – Micah (Micah 5:1-2)

18. B – A great army (Joel 2)

19. C – Samuel (1 Samuel 2:12-3:21)

20. False; in the New Testament, John the Baptist was also a prophet (Luke 1:76).

DID YOU KNOW?

- The time period of the books of the prophets in the Old Testament is roughly 400 years and covers the warnings to Israel, the exile, and the promise of restoration.

- The books of the prophets are commonly classified into two categories: major prophets and minor prophets. These distinctions simply mean that the major prophets wrote much more text. The minor prophets were originally all grouped together in one scroll. Fittingly, there are twelve minor prophets.

- The major prophets are Jeremiah, Isaiah, Daniel, and Ezekiel. The minor prophets are Hosea, Obadiah, Haggai, Nahum, Joel, Jonah, Habakkuk, Amos, Micah, Zechariah, Zephaniah, and Malachi.

- Prophecy in the Bible usually had an initial fulfillment as well as another distant, future fulfillment. This most likely happened so that those who heard the original prophecy would believe God's words. For example, in the famous passage of Isaiah 7:14, Isaiah is told that a "virgin" or "young woman" will conceive a child as a sign. This prophecy points forward to Christ but also to the next chapter in Isaiah when the prophet himself also receives a son.

- The prophetic legacies of the prophet Elijah and his student Elisha were very similar. Elijah literally passed down his mantle (cloak) to Elisha as he was taken up into Heaven, and Elisha followed closely in his footsteps. They both participated in a miracle involving a widow and her son; they both raised a child from the dead; and they both parted the Jordan river.
- The Bible records twice as many miracles during Elisha's life and ministry as during Elijah's, fulfilling Elisha's blessing to receive a "double portion."
- 2020's most searched and saved verse on the Bible app was Isaiah 41:10: "So do not fear, for I am with you; do not be dismayed, for I am your God. I will strengthen you and help you; I will uphold you with my righteous right hand."
- The bones of Elisha apparently held a special power. According to 2 Kings 13:21, they once raised a dead man back to life when he was thrown on them in burial.
- Jonah was a prophet from Galilee who took a message of repentance to Gentiles, and whose experience in the whale mirrored Christ's death, burial, and resurrection. It's no wonder Jesus compared Himself to Jonah in Matthew 12.
- Isaiah prophesied during the time of the kings in the same time period as Hosea and Micah. He was a

prophet to the Southern Kingdom of Judah during the time that the Northern Kingdom of Israel fell, and he warned Judah of their similar fate and upcoming judgment many decades in the future.

- Hosea's entire life, from his troubled marriage to the names of his children, was one big object lesson for the people of Israel. The names of his three children with the unfaithful Gomer were: Zereel meaning "God Scatters," Lo-Ruhamah meaning "Not Pitied," and Lo-Ammi meaning "Not My People."

- The prophet Jeremiah had a rough life. He was not permitted to marry; he was regularly persecuted and survived numerous attempts on his life; and he had the sad task of prophesying the impending destruction of Jerusalem.

- The prophet Daniel was taken to Babylon as a teenager during the exile and given the Babylonian name "Belteshazzar." He eventually rose to the third position of power in the kingdom under King Nabonidus. Portions of Daniel are in Aramaic.

- One overlooked fact about Daniel is that he was part of Judah's royal line! Perhaps this explains why he was taken captive and then selected to be a part of the palace court in Babylon.

- Despite most artistic interpretations to the contrary, Daniel was likely in his eighties when he was thrown into the lion's den during King Darius's reign.

- Like Daniel, Ezekiel was also taken to Babylon when he was young. He prophesied around the same time as Daniel did and began around the time that Jeremiah's ministry was ending.
- Zechariah, in a reverse of many of the other prophets, was born in Babylon but was brought back to Jerusalem with his family in the first wave of returns under Zerubbabel. He prophesied during the time of the construction of the second temple and immediately afterward to encourage the people and prepare them for the message of the coming Messiah.

THE NEW TESTAMENT

CHAPTER 6:
THE GOSPELS

TRIVIA TIME!

1. Which book starts with this famous line? "In the beginning was the Word and the Word was with God and the Word was God."

    a. Matthew
    b. Mark
    c. Luke
    d. John

2. Where was Matthew when he was called to follow Jesus and become a disciple of Christ?

    a. Tax booth
    b. Fishing boat
    c. Shores of Galilee
    d. At the Jordan River with John the Baptist

3. Which Gospel author was not Jewish?

    a. Matthew
    b. Mark

c. Luke
d. John

4. Which of these is not one of the Synoptic Gospels?
    a. Matthew
    b. Mark
    c. Luke
    d. John

5. Jesus fasted for this many days in the wilderness, paralleling the number of years the Israelites wandered:
    a. Seven
    b. Twelve
    c. Thirty
    d. Forty

6. True or false: Many of the twelve disciples were married when they began following Christ.

7. According to the Gospel of John, this disciple was the first one called:
    a. Simon Peter
    b. Matthew
    c. John
    d. Andrew

8. Jesus and the Holy Family resided in all of the following places except:
    a. Jerusalem
    b. Nazareth

c. Bethlehem

d. Egypt

9. Which of these is the shortest verse in the whole Bible?

   a. Jesus ran.
   b. Jesus wept.
   c. Jesus slept.
   d. Jesus spoke.

10. Who asked for John the Baptist's head on a platter?

    a. King Herod
    b. Herodias
    c. Salome
    d. Pilate

11. Peter first identified Jesus as the Christ at this location:

    a. Mount Hebron
    b. Caesarea Philippi
    c. The Jordan River
    d. Jerusalem

12. The tomb that Jesus was placed in belonged to whom?

    a. Joseph of Arimathea
    b. Mary and Martha
    c. Lazarus
    d. A gardener

13. Why did Pontius Pilate send Roman soldiers to guard Jesus's tomb?

    a. He was afraid grave robbers would take Jesus's clothes
    b. He knew Jesus had prophesied of His return
    c. He wanted to prove the disciples wrong
    d. He was afraid the people would protest

14. How did Judas betray Jesus in the Garden of Gethsemane?

    a. With a kiss
    b. With a sword
    c. With a hug
    d. With a nod

15. Which of these is not a line in the famous Beatitudes?

    a. Blessed are the meek, for they shall inherit the earth.
    b. Blessed are the merciful, for they shall obtain mercy.
    c. Blessed are the ones who are loved by God, for they shall see His face.
    d. Blessed are the peacemakers, for they shall be called sons of God.

16. What did Jesus's disciples call Him?

    a. Teacher
    b. Master
    c. Rabbi
    d. All of the above

17. What did Judas receive for betraying Christ?
    a. A vineyard
    b. A field
    c. Thirty pieces of silver
    d. Nothing

18. True or false: Peter and Andrew were the only pair of brothers of the twelve disciples.

19. Which Gospel author is said to have received his account from Peter?
    a. Matthew
    b. Mark
    c. Luke
    d. John

20. What did Zacchaeus do after encountering Jesus?
    a. Climbed a tree
    b. Left everything to follow Him
    c. Sold everything he had
    d. Gave back all he had exploited from the people

ANSWERS

1. D – John (John 1:1)
2. A – Tax booth (Matthew 9:9-13)
3. C – Luke (Colossians 4:10-14)
4. D – John
5. D – Forty (Matthew 4:1-11)
6. False; the only recorded reference to any of the disciples having a spouse is that of Peter's mother-in-law (Matthew 8:14).
7. D – Andrew (John 1:40-42)
8. A – Jerusalem (Matthew 12:2-23)
9. B – Jesus wept (John 11:35).
10. C – Salome (Matthew 14:8)
11. B – Caesarea Philippi (Matthew 16:13-20)
12. A – Joseph of Arimathea (Matthew 27:57-60)
13. B – He knew Jesus had prophesied of His return (Matthew 27:62).
14. A – With a kiss (Luke 22)
15. C – Blessed are the ones who are loved by God, for they shall see His face (Matthew 5:1-12).
16. D – All of the above (John 13:13, Matthew 23:7-8)

17. C – Thirty pieces of silver (Matthew 26:14-16)

18. False; James and John were brothers, and there were possibly more pairs as well.

19. B – Mark

20. D – If you answered (A), you were close as he did climb a tree to see Jesus before actually meeting him. The correct answer is (D), though, he gave back all he had exploited from the people (Luke 19:1-10).

DID YOU KNOW?

- Each of the Gospels focuses on Christ from a different angle. Matthew takes great care to show Christ as the fulfillment of Old Testament prophecy; John places emphasis on Christ as the Son of God; Luke focuses on Christ as the Son of Man; and Mark largely presents Christ as the Suffering Servant.

- While it is the subject of much debate, most scholars agree that the Gospel of Mark was likely written first, with Matthew shortly after, followed by Luke, and then John. All of the Gospels were dated to sometime in the first century, likely before the destruction of the temple in 70 AD.

- John uses the title "the disciple who Jesus loved" to refer to himself many times throughout his Gospel, most likely out of humility and reverence for Christ.

- Contrary to popular belief, scripture never says there were three wise men who came to visit Jesus after His birth, only that they brought three types of gifts. It is very likely that there were more than three who came to visit Him. In addition, they likely came many months after Jesus's birth since King Herod's response to the news was a decree to kill any male child under the age of two, not just newborns.

- In addition, many scholars believe Jesus was born in a shepherd's cave or on the lower floor of a house where animals were kept, not a stable as is commonly depicted. Lastly, for many years scholars have debated whether or not Jesus was born in December! However, there is no evidence of the date of Jesus's birth one way or the other. Regardless of whether it looked like our traditional nativity scenes today, it was a miracle either way.

- When Mary's forty-day period of purification was over, and the Holy Family went to present their sacrifice at the temple, we can see a hint at their financial status. A provision in the law stated that families who could not afford a lamb could offer a pair of turtledoves or pigeons instead. Luke 2:24 states that Mary and Joseph elected for the pair of birds for their sacrifice in accordance with the law, implying they were a family of modest means.

- The angel Gabriel was sent to both Zechariah and to Mary with news of a baby (John and Jesus, respectively). Zechariah and Mary both respond with a question, but Mary is praised while Zechariah is rebuked for his unbelief and is made mute until the prophecy is fulfilled. Why? Mary's question was from shock and curiosity, while Zechariah's was from unbelief.

- Most of the disciples were likely teenagers when they were called to follow the Rabbi Jesus, and in fact, it's speculated John was as young as thirteen!

- Many of the disciples had nicknames, and some are quite humorous. For example, Mark 3:17 records that the brothers James and John were affectionately called the "Sons of Thunder," probably for their boisterous personalities. Thomas was called "the twin." And most famously, Simon Peter gained the second half of his moniker with the addition of the Aramaic nickname "Cephas," which means "rock."

- The betrayal of Jesus is not the only shortcoming that scripture records about Judas. In John 12:6, we learn that "having charge of the moneybag, he used to help himself to what was put into it."

- The Last Supper was actually a Passover meal. Jesus shared this time of celebration with His disciples on the night before He was killed, in an event filled with symbolism. When He broke the bread and drank the wine, He was observing traditional elements of the Passover meal and explaining to the disciples how they pointed to Him.

- Jesus also celebrated Hanukkah (or at least went up to the temple for it). John 10:22-23 reads, "At that time the Feast of Dedication took place at Jerusalem. It was winter, and Jesus was walking in the temple, in the colonnade of Solomon."

- Nicodemus is most famous for his secret visit to Jesus in the night, where he inquired what it meant to be born again. However, this prominent Pharisee also appears in scripture at the burial of Jesus, where he donates a generous portion of embalming spices and assists Joseph of Arimathea with the burial. He also publicly defended Christ in front of the Sanhedrin in John 7.
- According to church tradition, all of the twelve disciples except for John were eventually martyred and killed for their faith. The scripture records one of these in Acts 12:2, where it notes that James was executed by King Herod with a sword.

CHAPTER 7:
ACTS

TRIVIA TIME!

1. Which disciple raised Tabatha from the dead?

    a. John
    b. Matthew
    c. Peter
    d. Paul

2. Who healed Paul after his conversion experience?

    a. Cornelius
    b. Ananias
    c. Peter
    d. Jesus

3. In which city did the term "Christians" first come about?

    a. Damascus
    b. Jerusalem
    c. Corinth
    d. Antioch

4. This man wanted to buy and capitalize on the gifts of the Holy Spirit:

    a. Simon the Sorcerer
    b. Philip
    c. Ananias
    d. Herod

5. True or false: Paul was imprisoned nine times.

6. Who was the first Christian martyr stoned under the supervision of Paul?

    a. Peter
    b. Silas
    c. Stephen
    d. Timothy

7. Who took Judas's place as one of the twelve disciples?

    a. Barnabas
    b. Matthias
    c. Paul
    d. Silas

8. True or false: Acts was written to tell us about the miracles of Jesus.

9. This disciple was led by the Holy Spirit to meet and baptize an Ethiopian eunuch on the road:

    a. Peter
    b. Paul
    c. Philip
    d. John

10. How did Peter escape from prison in Acts 12?
    a. The disciples broke him out
    b. His singing caused an earthquake
    c. His jailer had a change of heart
    d. An angel led him out

11. How did Paul and Silas react to their imprisonment in Acts 16?
    a. They prayed and sang hymns to God
    b. They cried
    c. They counted down the days on the prison wall
    d. They preached to all the prisoners

12. True or false: Paul was born a citizen of Rome.

13. Where was Paul shipwrecked on the way to Rome?
    a. Cyprus
    b. Malta
    c. Tarshish
    d. Patmos

14. Which of these was not a destination Paul visited on his missionary journeys?
    a. Rome
    b. Ephesus
    c. Damascus
    d. Patmos

15. True or false: A man once fell out of a window while Paul was preaching.

16. True or false: Paul participated in throwing stones at Stephen.

17. How many days after Jesus's resurrection did the disciples have to wait to receive the Holy Spirit?

    a. Seven days
    b. Ten days
    c. Forty days
    d. Fifty days

18. Where was Paul traveling to when he encountered the risen Jesus on the road?

    a. Damascus
    b. Rome
    c. Jerusalem
    d. Tarsus

19. Why did the masters of a young girl become angry with Paul and Silas in Acts 16?

    a. They tried to convert her
    b. They wanted to buy her back
    c. They had forgotten to pay her for their meal
    d. They cast out a spirit of divination from her, hurting their income

20. When Paul was shipwrecked, which animal should have hurt him but didn't?

    a. Lion
    b. Viper
    c. Tiger
    d. Scorpion

ANSWERS

1. C – Peter (Acts 9 32-34)
2. A – Cornelius (Acts 10)
3. D – Antioch (Acts 11:26
4. A – Simon the Sorcerer (Acts 8:9-24)
5. False; although the Bible speaks of many times that Paul was accused or taken into custody, he was only placed in jail three times that the Bible speaks of. All together, Paul spent about five years of his life imprisoned.
6. C – Stephen (Acts 7:54-60)
7. B – Matthias (Acts 1:16-20)
8. False; Acts was written to give an account of the "acts of the Apostles."
9. C – Philip (Acts 8:34-39)
10. D – An angel led him out (Acts 12:8).
11. A – They prayed and sang hymns to God (Acts 16:25).
12. True; Paul used his Roman citizenship to get out of harsher punishment (Acts 28:1-31).
13. B – Malta (Acts 27)
14. D – Patmos (Acts 23:11, Acts 19, Acts 9:1-19)

15. True; in Acts 20:9, a young man named Eutychus fell asleep and fell out of a window. After he apparently died, Paul revived him back to life.

16. False; although he was present, Paul was holding the killers' coats (Acts 7:54-60).

17. D – Fifty days (Acts 2:1-4)

18. A – Damascus (Acts 9:5)

19. D – They cast out a spirit of divination from her, hurting their income (Acts 16:16).

20. B – Viper (Acts 28:1-10)

DID YOU KNOW?

- The book of Acts starts with Jesus's last words to His disciples and tells the story of them carrying out His instructions: "You will receive power when the Holy Spirit has come upon you, and you will be my witnesses in Jerusalem and in all Judea and Samaria, and to the end of the earth." (Acts 1:8)

- Luke and Acts both open with a greeting to a man named Theophilus. Luke wrote these books for this mysterious friend who most scholars agree was probably a prominent Roman official or another influential Gentile.

- Luke was a doctor and a close companion to Paul during many of his travels. It is believed Luke was a Gentile because when Paul lists his Jewish companions in Colossians 4:10-11, he does not mention Luke as being "of the circumcision" despite the context insinuating Luke was present. However, this is never outright specified in the Bible. To write the book of Luke, he compiled many eyewitness accounts to tell the whole story of Christ with precision and detail. As a well-educated and observant man, his efforts to write down the events of Christ's life and the history of the early church resulted in his Gospel account as well as the book of Acts that still benefit us today.

- Although Paul often gets credit for writing the largest portion of the New Testament, Luke actually exceeds him in the number of words written. His two books (Luke and Acts) make up more than 37,000 words, while Paul's many writings make up just over 32,000 words. In fact, in the entire Bible, only Moses and Ezra contributed more to the total word count than Luke.

- Before his conversion, Paul studied under the great Gamaliel and was most likely either being primed for a spot on the Jewish council of the Sanhedrin or was already a member.

- From his position of high standing, we can also gather that Paul was most likely married at some point and possibly became a widower since there is evidence that having a wife was a requirement to be on the Sanhedrin. Although we cannot say for certain, many scholars believe this was the case.

- Paul is also known by the Hebrew version of his name, Saul of Tarsus: "Saul, who was also called Paul" (Acts 13:9). It was standard practice at the time to have two names. It is likely that he was known as either Paul or Saul, depending on the native tongue of the speaker. Paul is simply a Roman way of saying Saul and would have been an easier name for Gentiles to pronounce. For the man who strived to be "all things to all people," it makes sense that he would become known by both his Hebrew name and his Roman one over time. However, some scholars believe choosing the name Paul over Saul is an act of humility, as Paul means "little" and Saul means "desired."

- Paul's missionary journeys took him through modern-day Syria, Turkey, and Greece. His three major trips lasted a combined nine years and were comprised of more than 5,000 miles. In total, it is said that he probably spent as many as twenty years of his life on the road or in prison spreading the good news of Christ.

- The two main figures of the book of Acts are Peter and Paul, with them both being active in bringing the Gospel to the Gentiles. Peter was the first to convert a Gentile, a centurion named Cornelius, after which the Jewish converts were amazed and glorified God.

- Peter preached the first major evangelistic sermon at the Upper Room on Pentecost. Scripture records that more than 3,000 people became believers in Christ on that day.

- Many miracles were recorded in the book of Acts, including the resurrection of Tabitha (Dorcas) by Peter in Joppa, the healing of a cripple by Paul in Lystra, and the healing of a lame man by Peter and John at the temple.

- In the time of the book of Acts, people believed in God's power to heal through Peter so strongly that many were healed simply by falling under his shadow or by touching handkerchiefs that he had touched.

CHAPTER 8:
PAUL'S EPISTLES

TRIVIA TIME!

1. In 1 Corinthians 16:14, Paul encourages his disciples to "Do everything with ____."

    a. Love
    b. Joy
    c. Peace
    d. Hope

2. Which of these is NOT an instruction that Paul gave to the early church?

    a. Beware of false teachers
    b. Don't be surprised when you encounter hardship
    c. The church must collect a tithe of 10% from each member
    d. Married women should have a head covering at church

3. In Hebrews 12, Paul implores Christians to run their race with:

a. Love
   b. Joy
   c. Peace
   d. Endurance

4. In Philippians 3:20, Paul says what about the citizenship of a believer?
   a. It is everlasting
   b. It cannot be taken away
   c. It was bought at a price
   d. It is in Heaven

5. True or false: After Paul prayed three times, God took away the "thorn in his side."

6. In addition to being a Pharisee and later a missionary preacher, Paul also was:
   a. A shoemaker
   b. A tent maker
   c. A fisherman
   d. A doctor

7. Which of these is NOT part of the "Armor of God" from Ephesians 6?
   a. The shoes of war
   b. The breastplate of righteousness
   c. The sword of the spirit
   d. The helmet of salvation

8. In 1 Corinthians, "in the twinkling of an eye, at the last trumpet," we shall be:

a. Alive
   b. Clothed
   c. Changed
   d. Asleep

9. True or false: Paul met and worked with some of the original twelve disciples.

10. Romans 1:16 reads, "For I am not ashamed of ____."
    a. God
    b. Christ
    c. The Gospel
    d. My friends

11. Which of these is NOT included in the famous 1 Corinthians 13 passage? Love is:
    a. Patient
    b. Kind
    c. Not boastful
    d. Wonderful

12. Complete this famous line: "O foolish Galatians, who has ____ you?"
    a. Bewitched
    b. Lied to
    c. Corrupted
    d. Preached to

13. According to Paul, Christians should avoid being "unequally yoked" to what?

a. A master
b. Money
c. Unbelievers
d. False teaching

14. In this letter, Paul had to reassure his followers that the Day of the Lord had not yet come:
    a. Corinthians
    b. Thessalonians
    c. Romans
    d. Hebrews

15. In Ephesians 5, husbands are called to love their wives:
    a. Like Christ loved the church
    b. Like God loves His children
    c. Like their wives love them
    d. Like the world loves money

16. In Ephesians 4, believers are called to deal with what emotion before the sun goes down?
    a. Love
    b. Hatred
    c. Jealousy
    d. Anger

17. Complete this famous line from Philippians 1:21: "For to me to live is Christ, and to die is ___."
    a. Fine
    b. Gain

c. Christ
   d. Live

18. 1 Thessalonians 5:17 says, "pray without ____."
   a. Ceasing
   b. Doubt
   c. Thinking
   d. Words

19. Which of these is NOT a "Fruit of the Spirit?"
   a. Love
   b. Joy
   c. Prayer
   d. Self-control

20. True or false: Paul had two sons, named Titus and Timothy.

ANSWERS

1. A – Love (1 Corinthians 16:14)
2. C – The church must collect a tithe of 10% from each member (1 Timothy 6:3-5, Romans 16:17-20, 2 Corinthians 6:3).
3. D – Endurance (Hebrews 12:1)
4. D – It is in Heaven (Philippians 3:20)
5. False; while we do not know what this thorn was, scripture says it was not taken away, but Paul learned to live with it in humility and with God's strength (2 Corinthians 12:7-9).
6. B – A tent-maker (Acts 18:3)
7. A – The shoes of war (Ephesians 6)
8. C – Changed (1 Corinthians 15:52)
9. True; Paul specifically mentions Peter and John and likely met others as well (Galatians 1:18-20).
10. C – The Gospel (Romans 1:16)
11. D – Wonderful (1 Corinthians 13)
12. A – Bewitched (Galatians 3:1)
13. C – Unbelievers (2 Corinthians 6:14)
14. B – Thessalonians (2 Thessalonians 2:2)

15. A – Like Christ loved the church (Ephesians 5:25)

16. D – Anger (Ephesians 4:26)

17. B – Gain (Philippians 1:21)

18. A – Ceasing (1 Thessalonians 5:17)

19. C – Prayer (Galatians 5:22-23)

20. False; Paul had no recorded sons, although Timothy was "like a son" to him (1 Timothy 1:2).

DID YOU KNOW?

- Martin Luther (and thus the Protestant Reformation) was heavily influenced by Paul's letters, especially Romans 1:17. This verse in the translations of Luther's day would have read something like "the one who by faith is righteous shall live."

- In the Bible, there are a total of thirteen verified letters of Paul to various congregations. These are Galatians, 1 and 2 Thessalonians, 1 and 2 Corinthians, Romans, Ephesians, Philemon, Colossians, Philippians, 1 and 2 Timothy, and Titus.

- Five of these letters (Ephesians, Philemon, Colossians, Philippians, and 2 Timothy) were penned by Paul while he was imprisoned in Rome!

- Paul's final words from his second imprisonment are recorded in 2 Timothy.

- It is often assumed that Paul also wrote the book of Hebrews, but it is not known for sure. It is possible Hebrews was a sermon Paul preached that Luke or another follower transcribed into a letter. Another suggestion with some weight behind it is that Hebrews was written by Apollos, an associate of Paul with knowledge of both Greek rhetoric and Jewish theology. No matter who wrote it, the book of

Hebrews is theologically rich and one of the most significant books of the Bible.

- Although none of Paul's other letters were written anonymously without a greeting, as Hebrews is, the book uses the same closing as Paul's letters ("Grace be with you,") mentions Timothy as did many of Paul's other letters, and has a similar message to Paul's writings.

- It is a little-known fact that Paul did not start his ministry right away. In fact, he apparently went off the scene and into a period of spiritual solitude for three years before ultimately meeting with Peter and James, the brother of Jesus, in Jerusalem, to kick off his travels (Galatians 1:17-21).

- While Paul was inarguably an excellent writer, he apparently was not as great at giving speeches, as evidenced by his own words in 1 and 2 Corinthians.

- Paul faced significant challenges throughout his missionary journeys, including being shipwrecked, imprisoned, and persecuted – sometimes by his own people.

- Paul was ultimately martyred in Rome under Nero. Although we do not know the exact date and manner of his death, church tradition is that he was beheaded.

CHAPTER 9:
OTHER LETTERS

TRIVIA TIME!

1. Finish this verse: "See what kind of love the Father has given to us, that we should be called _____." (1 John 3:1).

    a. Children of God
    b. Believers in Christ
    c. Adopted into God's family
    d. Grafted into Israel

2. Who wrote these words? "Beloved, let us love one another, for love is from God, and whoever loves has been born of God and knows God."

    a. Peter
    b. John
    c. Paul
    d. James

3. 1 Peter 4:12 encourages believers in Christ not to be surprised at what?

a. Fiery trials
   b. His second coming
   c. War
   d. Famine

4. Jude implores believers to "save others by ____."
   a. Baptizing them in the name of the Father, Son, and Holy Spirit
   b. Praying for them always
   c. Preaching to them the truth of righteousness
   d. Snatching them out of the fire

5. Which author wrote these famous words? "Resist the devil, and he will flee from you."
   a. Peter
   b. James
   c. John
   d. Jude

6. In John's letters, he frequently refers to the believers as:
   a. Brothers
   b. Elders
   c. Little children
   d. Sheep

7. Who is "like a man who looks intently at his natural face in a mirror" and "goes away and at once forgets what he was like" (James 1:23-24)?
   a. Unbelievers
   b. Anyone who does not pray

c. The one who hears the Word but does not do it
   d. King Herod

8. According to the book of James, "Religion that is pure and undefiled" is what?
   a. To follow God's law perfectly
   b. To pray without ceasing
   c. To love God with all your heart
   d. To care for orphans and widows

9. James made the famous statement that "faith without works is dead" because "even ___ believe and shudder."
   a. Kings
   b. Pharisees
   c. Demons
   d. Angels

10. Peter tells believers to always be ready "to make a defense to anyone who asks you for a reason for the ___ that is in you."
    a. Love
    b. Joy
    c. Peace
    d. Hope

11. Which body part does James liken to a ship's rudder and a torch of fire?
    a. The eyes
    b. The lips

c. The tongue
   d. The feet

12. Wives with husbands who "do not obey the word" were advised by Peter to:
    a. Pray for their souls
    b. Nag them until they repent
    c. Leave them
    d. Win them over with respectful and pure conduct

13. Which of these authors did not write a New Testament epistle?
    a. James
    b. Peter
    c. Philemon
    d. Jude

14. Jude quotes from which ancient prophet?
    a. Jeremiah
    b. Enoch
    c. Daniel
    d. Isaiah

15. According to 1 John 4:18, "Perfect love casts out ___."
    a. Fear
    b. Sin
    c. Death
    d. Shame

16. According to James, every good and perfect gift comes from ___?
    a. Prayer
    b. Hard work
    c. Love
    d. Our Father above

17. "If we say _____ we deceive ourselves, and the truth is not in us" (1 John 1:8).
    a. We love God
    b. We love others
    c. We have no sin
    d. We follow God's laws

18. True or false: According to James, we have just as much power in prayer as Elijah did when he stopped the rain.

19. Finish this famous quote: "The devil prowls around like a roaring ____."
    a. Tiger
    b. Lion
    c. Serpent
    d. Beast

20. True or false: Jude was the brother of James (and many say of Jesus as well).

ANSWERS

1. A – Children of God (1 John 3:1)
2. B – John (1 John 4:7)
3. A – Fiery trials (1 Peter 4:12)
4. D – Snatching them out of the fire (Jude 23)
5. B – James (James 4:7)
6. C – Little children (1 John 2:1)
7. C – The one who hears the Word but does not do it (Jams 1:23-24)
8. D – To care for orphans and widows (James 1:27)
9. C – Demons (James 2:17)
10. D – Hope (1 Peter 3:15)
11. C – The tongue (James 3:4-6)
12. D – Win them over with respectful and pure conduct (1 Peter 3)
13. C – Philemon
14. B – Enoch (Jude 1:14)
15. A – Fear (1 John 4:18)
16. D –Our Father above (James 1:17)
17. C – We have no sin (1 John 1:8)

18. True; after encouraging the believers about the power of prayer, James goes on to say that "Elijah was a man with a nature like ours"(James 5:13-18).

19. B – Lion (1 Peter 5:8)

20. True; James and Jude were brothers and, according to tradition, were also related to Jesus Himself (Jude 1:1).

DID YOU KNOW?

- After the resurrection and ascension of Christ, Peter and James and John became leaders of the early church community in Jerusalem (Galatians 2:9). So, it is no surprise that their letters are also included as part of the scriptures.
- 1 Peter 5:13 confirms Peter's close relationship with Mark, who reportedly wrote his Gospel under the teaching and influence of Peter.
- As we learned from the Gospel accounts, Peter was married, but did you know his wife often traveled with him? 1 Corinthians 9:5 confirms this.
- Perhaps one of the most notable accounts of Christian martyrdom is that of Peter. It is a common assumption that he, in honor of Jesus, refused an upright crucifixion and asked to be hung upside down instead
- Jude and James were described as initially failing to believe that Jesus was the Christ (Mark 3:21 and John 7:5). However, this obviously shifted after the resurrection, with both brothers going on to write their own epistles.
- Jude seems to be very well-read, as he referenced or quoted from various extra-Biblical writings such as Enoch and the Assumption of Moses.

- Jude is one of the few books of the New Testament that was not specifically directed to any one group or region of people.

- The book of James may have been written before any of Paul's letters, making it one of the earliest New Testament writings. It was written to Jewish believers.

- James was also known as "James the Just," due to his time spent in prayer.

- There were at least three different apostles named James in the early church period: James the son of Zebedee and brother of John who was one of the twelve disciples; James the brother of Jude and likely half-brother of Jesus; and James the son of Alphaeus, who was also called James the Less.

- According to several historians, James was martyred sometime in the 60s AD. He was thrown off the temple and stoned by the Jewish religious leaders. When the temple fell to the Romans a few years later, in 70 AD, many Jews saw it as judgment for James's death.

CHAPTER 10:
REVELATION

TRIVIA TIME!

1. In John's vision, which of these was he instructed not to write down because it was concealed for a later time?
   a. The seven bowls
   b. The seven trumpets
   c. The seven seals
   d. The seven thunders

2. In Revelation 20, Satan is bound and cast into the bottomless pit for:
   a. Seven years
   b. 1,000 years
   c. Forty days and nights
   d. Eternity

3. Which of these is not a church mentioned in the seven letters of Revelation?
   a. Ephesus
   b. Thyatira

c. Philadelphia
   d. Philippi
4. John wrote the book of Revelation from which island?
   a. Patmos
   b. Rome
   c. Crete
   d. Cyprus
5. In the book of Revelation, the golden bowls full of incense represent what?
   a. The fire of God's wrath
   b. The prayers of the Saints
   c. The blood of the sacrifices
   d. The lives of the martyrs
6. True or false: Revelation mentions the same beast seen in the book of Daniel.
7. There is an event that is described three times in the book of Revelation, once in each set of judgments. What is it?
   a. A fire
   b. A flood
   c. An earthquake
   d. A plague
8. Which of these is NOT one of the four horsemen of the Apocalypse?
   a. Death
   b. War

c. Famine
d. Disease

9. Which of these angels is mentioned by name in the book of Revelation?

   a. Gabriel
   b. Michael
   c. Raphael
   d. Uriel

10. John saw a vision of a Heavenly city. How many gates did it have?

    a. Four
    b. Seven
    c. Ten
    d. Twelve

11. In Revelation 22, where is the tree of life?

    a. In the throne room
    b. On either side of the river
    c. In the middle of the garden
    d. Growing in the river

12. What is the name of the city that comes down from Heaven like a bride?

    a. Jerusalem
    b. Babylon
    c. Eden
    d. Shiloh

13. True or false: The angels sing a special song around the throne.

14. In Revelation 5, the lamb was the only one who was worthy to:
    a. Open the scroll
    b. Pour out the bowls
    c. Sound the trumpet
    d. Ride the white horse

15. In Revelation 6:10, the souls under the altar cry out:
    a. "Holy, Holy, Holy is the Lord God Almighty!"
    b. "How long?"
    c. "Worthy is the Lamb!"
    d. "Where is the Lord?"

16. As mentioned in Revelation 8:10-11, what is wormwood?
    a. An angel
    b. A river
    c. A disease
    d. A star

17. The seven churches are represented in the book of Revelation as what:
    a. Seven lampstands
    b. Seven stars
    c. Seven angels
    d. Seven scrolls

18. According to Revelation 19:16, what is on Jesus's thigh?

   a. A sword
   b. Flaming fire
   c. Blood
   d. A name is written: King of Kings and Lord of Lords

19. The twelve gates of Heaven (New Jerusalem) are made of what?

   a. Gold
   b. Fine linen
   c. Pearls
   d. Gemstones

20. True or false: Jesus told one church, "I will spit you out of my mouth."

ANSWERS

1. D – The seven thunders (Revelation 10:4)
2. B – 1,000 years (Revelation 20:1)
3. D – Philippi (Revelation 2:1, 2:18, 3:7-13)
4. A – Patmos (Revelation 1:9)
5. B – The prayers of the Saints (Revelation 5:8)
6. True; the beast described in Revelation contains elements of all Daniel's beasts (Daniel 7:5, Revelation 13:1-2).
7. C – An earthquake (Revelation 11:13, Revelation 16:18, Revelation 6:12)
8. D – Disease (Revelation 6:1-8)
9. B – Michael (Revelation 12:7)
10. D – Twelve (Revelation 21:12)
11. B – On either side of the river (Revelation 22:2)
12. A – Jerusalem (Revelation 21:2)
13. True; in many places in the book of Revelation, angels and living creatures are described as singing praises to God (Revelation 5:11).
14. A – Open the scroll (Revelation 5)
15. B – "How long?" (Revelation 6:10)

16. D – A star (Revelation 8:10-11)

17. A – Seven lampstands (Revelation 1:20)

18. D – A name written: King of Kings and Lord of Lords (Revelation 19:16)

19. C – Pearls (Revelation 21:11)

20. True; the church at Laodicea was rebuked for being lukewarm (Revelation 3:16).

DID YOU KNOW?

- The word "Revelation" comes from a Greek word which means "a revealing or disclosure."

- Revelation is written in Greek, in a style some scholars believe to be different than that of John's Gospel. However, this difference could be easily explained in that John had the help of a fluent scribe for his Gospel, whereas in exile he had to pen his writings himself.

- The book of Revelation was addressed to the "seven churches of Asia" which include: Ephesus, Smyrna, Pergamum, Thyatira, Sardis, Philadelphia, and Laodicea. All of these churches were located in modern-day Turkey and along a major Roman road. Of these, it appears the church at Philadelphia was the most faithful.

- Though there is debate about exactly when Revelation was written, scholarly consensus largely places it somewhere between 90-95 AD. It is believed that John was around the age of ninety years old when the book was written.

- During the time the book of Revelation was written, Christians were under very heavy persecution from the Roman emperor Domitian who reigned from 81-

96 AD. It is believed this is partly the reason for the symbolic language used in the book of Revelation— to cover political figures and events in obscurity in case the letter to the Christians was intercepted.

- There are more than two hundred references to concepts or verses from the Old Testament in the book of Revelation. This also contributes to making Revelation a very complex and complicated book to understand. The book has been subject to much misinterpretation over the years and many of its symbolic meanings are still hotly contested today.

- Besides the famous "666" that represents the "mark of the beast," Revelation includes many other key numbers such as the seven groups of judgements, the 144,000 sealed Israelites, the ten kings associated with the beast, and the 1,260 days that Israel will be protected in the wilderness.

- Revelation reverses or complements much of what is written in Genesis. For example, Genesis records the fall of mankind while Revelation records the redemption of mankind. Genesis records the beginning of death and Revelation records the end of death.

- John was banished to the island of Patmos at the end of his life for his work preaching the Gospel. Many historians believe that John died a natural death there on the island or perhaps elsewhere after writing the book of Revelation. He was the only one of the twelve disciples who was not martyred.

- Revelation 22:18-19 carries a cryptic warning about those who would tamper with the message of the book: "I warn everyone who hears the words of the prophecy of this book: if anyone adds to them, God will add to him the plagues described in this book, and if anyone takes away from the words of the book of this prophecy, God will take away his share in the tree of life and in the holy city, which are described in this book."

- In a very fitting conclusion, the last word of the entire Bible in Revelation 22:21 is "amen." The word amen means "so be it" and has its origination in the Hebrew scriptures, although Revelation was written in Greek.

- Revelation is the only apocalyptic or prophetic book in the entire New Testament.

ABOUT THE BIBLE

CHAPTER 11:

WOMEN IN THE BIBLE

TRIVIA TIME!

1. Esther was raised by her cousin ____.
    a. Haman
    b. Mordecai
    c. Vashti
    d. Hathach

2. True or false: Ruth had a sister-in-law who chose to go home to her parents instead of with Naomi back to Israel.

3. Naomi wanted to change her name to a word meaning what?
    a. Bitter
    b. Sorrow
    c. Hunger
    d. Famine

4. Deborah famously told which man that victory would come from a woman?

a. Sisera
   b. Barak
   c. Jabin
   d. Heber

5. What was the name of Abigail's first husband, who acted wrongly towards King David and his men?
   a. Haman
   b. Naaman
   c. Nabal
   d. Michal

6. What did Eli think when he first saw Hannah praying in the temple?
   a. That she was a righteous woman
   b. That she was a widow
   c. That she was drunk
   d. That her prayers would be answered

7. True or false: After their mother placed him in the water, a young Miriam followed baby Moses to see which way he would go.

8. Mary & Martha were:
   a. Friends
   b. Sisters
   c. Cousins
   d. Rival wives

9. True or false: The widow Anna who lived at the temple was the only one to recognize Christ.

10. Lydia of Thyatira, who was encountered by Paul on his missionary journeys, was a seller of what?

    a. Shoes
    b. Oils and spices
    c. Fortune telling
    d. Purple goods

11. The mother of these two disciples famously asked Jesus if her sons could sit on His right and left in the Kingdom:

    a. Andrew and Peter
    b. James and John
    c. Judas and Simon
    d. Thaddeus and Matthew

12. Hagar gave this name to God after fleeing from Abraham and Sarah and being encouraged by an angel in the wilderness:

    a. The God Who Saves
    b. The God Who Sees
    c. The God Who Loves
    d. The God Who Cares

13. Who told Mary, "Blessed are you among women, and blessed is the fruit of your womb?"

    a. Elizabeth
    b. The angel Gabriel
    c. Joseph
    d. Simeon

14. To whom did Christ assign the care of his mother when He was on the cross?
    a. John
    b. Peter
    c. James
    d. Mary Magdalene

15. True or false: Rachel and Leah once had a famous argument over a plant.

16. Rebekah was selected to be the wife of Isaac when she:
    a. Got off her camel to greet him
    b. Offered water to his servant's camels
    c. Traveled many miles to meet Abraham
    d. Was born to Isaac's relative

17. Mary Magdalene got her name from:
    a. The town that she was from
    b. A demon that was cast out of her
    c. The color of her hair
    d. The name of her ex-husband

18. What did Rahab need to lower out of her window in order to be saved from the Israelite army?
    a. A red rope
    b. Her hair
    c. A white sheet
    d. A white flag

19. True or false: Mary was told in a prophecy that "a sword will pierce your own soul."

20. Prior to becoming Queen, Esther underwent beauty treatments for how long?
    a. One month
    b. Forty days
    c. Six months
    d. One year

ANSWERS

1. B – Mordecai (Esther 2:7)
2. True; her name was Orpah (Ruth 1:15).
3. A – Bitter (Ruth 1:20)
4. B – Barak (Judges 4:9)
5. C – Nabal (1 Samuel 25:3)
6. C – That she was drunk (1:13)
7. True; she watched as Pharaoh's daughter drew him out of the river (Exodus 2:4).
8. B – Sisters (Luke 10:38-42)
9. False; an elderly man named Simeon also had this truth revealed to him by God (Luke 2:36-40).
10. D – Purple goods (Acts 16:14)
11. B – James and John (Matthew 20:20-21)
12. B – The God Who Sees (Genesis 12:13)
13. A – Elizabeth (Luke 1:42)
14. A – John (19:25-27)
15. True; the women both wanted the mandrake root for fertility purposes (Genesis 30:16).
16. B – Offered water to his servant's camels (Genesis 24)
17. A – The town that she was from

18. A – A red rope (Joshua 2:15)

19. True; this is part of the prophecy told to Mary and Joseph by Simeon at the time of the presentation of Jesus at the temple (Luke 2:35).

20. D – One year (Esther 2:12)

DID YOU KNOW?

- There are more than one hundred women named in the Bible, and ninety-three who speak. Women are extremely important to God's story and are often shown being treated with the utmost respect by Jesus and others. Some women were military heroes, some were judges or prophets, others were influential women of great financial means, and still others were the mothers of very important Biblical figures. But they all had a role to play.

- There are female villains in the Bible too! Some of the most notable are the evil Queen Jezebel who sought to kill the prophet Elijah, Queen Herodias who tricked her husband into killing John the Baptist, and the whore of Babylon mentioned in Revelation.

- By God's providence, not only did Moses's mother save his life by placing him in the basket, but she also got to nurse him too! When Pharaoh's daughter found the baby in the river, she decided to adopt him as her own, but she needed a nursemaid. Moses's own mother was (probably unknowingly) hired for the task.

- While Deborah often gets all the credit as the heroine in the battle against King Jabin, there was actually another woman named Jael who singlehandedly killed Sisera (the commander of the Canaanite army) with a tent peg.

- The book of Esther is the only book that doesn't specifically mention God; however, that does not mean God is absent from the story. God's providential hand is shown throughout the events of the book, and mention is also made of prayer and fasting.

- Interestingly, Esther is also the only book in the Biblical canon NOT found with the Dead Sea Scrolls. Perhaps this lends some credibility to the theory that the caves could have been a repository of sorts for old scrolls containing the name of God that the ancient Jews did not wish to burn or discard in another way.

- The book of Ruth takes place in Bethlehem during the time of the Judges. As part of the lineage of Christ, it makes sense that Ruth and Boaz would have their home there. Many generations later, Joseph would return to this land of his ancestors to report for the census with his young pregnant bride.

- In the book of Ruth, Boaz and another family member complete a real estate transaction with the giving of a shoe. But why a shoe? This custom, which could be likened to the simple business handshake of today, likely originated from one of two ancient thoughts. In that day, one would remove their shoes upon entering a home to cleanse their feet, thus potentially signifying ownership or at least residence of a property. Also, it was largely thought that he who was first to "set foot" on a property had the right to acquire it, making the giving of a shoe perhaps a most fitting gesture after all.

- The story of Queen Esther has inspired many books and movies. But did you know she also was behind the creation of a Jewish holiday still celebrated today? Purim is celebrated in Jewish communities by reading the book of Esther, sending gifts to one another, giving to the poor, feasting with family and friends, and of course "booing" the wicked Haman. It is also customary to dress up in costumes and masks on this day.

- Anna is one of the few female prophetesses named in the Bible and the only one in the New Testament. She was a widow who spent all her time at the temple and was enabled by the Holy Spirit to recognize the baby Jesus as the Son of God.

- In the days before ultrasounds, Rebekah was so confused by her twin sons jostling around in her womb that she sought out prophecy from the Lord to understand what was going on. This is where she learned, "Two nations are in your womb, and two peoples from within you shall be divided; the one shall be stronger than the other, the older shall serve the younger" (Genesis 25:23).

- Abraham's wife Sarah was the only woman in the Bible to have her name changed. God changed her name from Sarai, which means "my princess," to Sarah, which means "mother of nations."

- There are four important songs or hymns of prayer attributed to women in the Bible: The Song of Miriam, The Song of Deborah, The Song of Hannah, and Mary's Magnificat.

- Some of the most underrated Bible heroines are the midwives in Egypt who saved the Hebrew babies. Shiphrah and Puah refused to follow the Pharaoh's instruction to kill newborn Jewish boys and are later rewarded by God for their faithfulness. These women risked their lives, allowing for baby Moses (among many others) to be born. Not bad for a day's work!

- Bathsheba played an important role in persuading her husband (King David) to appoint her son Solomon as the next in line for the throne. Without her, we may not have had the book of Proverbs or the first Jewish temple!

CHAPTER 12:
BIBLE HEROES

TRIVIA TIME!

1. Samson's strength came from which of the following items?

    a. His cloak
    b. His staff
    c. His hair
    d. His shoes

2. With what did David kill Goliath?

    a. A large stone
    b. 5 smooth stones
    c. A sword
    d. A bow and arrow

3. Moses was afraid to answer the call of God because:

    a. He was not good at speaking
    b. He could not read or write
    c. He was scared of Pharaoh
    d. He didn't want to leave his wife

4. Who told Esther these famous words: "And who knows whether you have not come to the kingdom for such a time as this?"
   a. King Xerxes
   b. The palace eunuch
   c. Haman
   d. Mordecai

5. Joshua is most famous for:
   a. Leading the Israelites in battle and into the Promised Land
   b. Leading the Israelites out of Egypt
   c. Leading the Israelites during the forty years in the wilderness
   d. Leading the Israelites in their land until King Saul came about

6. True or false: Nehemiah is credited with rebuilding the city of Jerusalem.

7. True or false: Joseph never forgave his brothers for selling him into slavery.

8. It took Noah this long to build the Ark:
   a. Weeks
   b. Months
   c. Years
   d. Decades

9. Abraham was told his descendants would become:

a. As numerous as the stars in the sky and the sand on the seashore
   b. A nation of kings
   c. The Jewish people
   d. A kingdom of priests

10. Hebrews Chapter 11 is often called what:
    a. Hall of Fame
    b. Hall of Heroes
    c. Hall of Faith
    d. Hall of Legends

11. Samson once killed a lion with:
    a. A rock
    b. A slingshot
    c. A knife
    d. His bare hands

12. What did Moses often use to show his signs to Pharaoh and the people?
    a. Fire
    b. His staff
    c. A snake
    d. His cloak

13. How did Samson destroy the fields of the Philistines?
    a. Set them on fire by tying torches to the tails of foxes
    b. Trampled on them with his strength
    c. Flooded them with water from the Jordan River
    d. Led his army to carry out a battle there

14. What is the best meaning for the word Messiah?
    a. Savior
    b. King
    c. Anointed
    d. God

15. How did Joseph eventually gain his freedom from prison?
    a. He interpreted a dream for Pharaoh
    b. He interpreted a dream for Pharaoh's cupbearer
    c. He proved his innocence in court
    d. He was released due to a national famine

16. How did Daniel get out of the lion's den?
    a. He fasted and prayed for three days
    b. He asked the king to let him out early
    c. God miraculously shut the lion's mouth
    d. An angel stood with him and protected him

17. What did Shadrach, Meshach, and Abednego do to get thrown into the fiery furnace?
    a. They prayed three times a day to God
    b. They refused to bow down before the king
    c. They could not interpret the king's dream
    d. They were caught stealing a golden cup from the king's palace

18. True or false: Deborah was the only female judge mentioned in the Bible.

19. What did the prophet Samuel think when he heard God's voice for the first time?
    a. That his master was calling him
    b. That he was having a dream
    c. That he was selected to be the next king
    d. That he should go back to sleep
20. True or false: David was a child when he killed Goliath.

ANSWERS

1. C – His hair (Judges 13:24-25)
2. B – Five smooth stones (1 Samuel 17)
3. A – He was not good at speaking (Exodus 3:11-13)
4. D – Mordecai (Esther 4:14)
5. A – Leading the Israelites in battle and into the Promised Land (Joshua 1-24)
6. True; he is best known for helping rebuild the city walls, thus protecting the city (Nehemiah 2:20).
7. False; Joseph forgave his brothers, famously saying "You meant evil against me, but God meant it for good, to bring it about that many people should be kept alive… (50:15-21)"
8. D – Decades (Genesis 7:11)
9. A – As numerous as the stars in the sky and the sand on the seashore (Genesis 26:4)
10. C – Hall of Faith (Hebrews 11)
11. D – His bare hands (Judges 14:5)
12. B – His staff (Exodus 4:3)
13. A – Set them on fire by tying torches to the tails of foxes (Judges 15:14-16)
14. C – Anointed

15. A – He interpreted a dream for Pharaoh (Genesis 41)

16. C – God miraculously shut the lion's mouth (Daniel 6:21)

17. B – They refused to bow down before the king (Daniel 3:18)

18. True; while other prominent women are included in the Bible, Deborah was the only female judge of Israel that we know of (Judges 4).

19. A – That his master was calling him (1 Samuel 3:4-11)

20. True; David was most likely a teenager when he killed Goliath since he was too young to fight with his brothers when they left for war (1 Samuel 17).

DID YOU KNOW?

- David had to wait many years (some scholars believe it was more than two decades) before becoming king! The prevailing view among scholars is that David was anointed by the prophet Samuel as a young boy or teenager, and later spent many years on the run from King Saul before finally taking the throne somewhere around the age of thirty.

- King Darius was greatly troubled when Daniel was thrown in the lion's den. He was tricked by his officials who sought to get rid of Daniel and his position over them. Daniel 6:20 records that in the morning, King Darius hurried to the den and cried out in anguish, "O Daniel, servant of the living God, has your God, whom you serve continually, been able to deliver you from the lions?" When he saw that Daniel was alive, he was overjoyed and ordered the execution of those who had accused him instead.

- In both the book of Esther and the book of Daniel, those who sought to persecute a righteous Jew were themselves killed with the same instrument of torture they had devised. The wicked Haman is hung on the gallows he prepared for Mordecai, and Daniel's accusers were later thrown into the lion's den after he was delivered from death. God brought each of these events about to show His perfect justice for those who seek to harm His people.

- Both Abraham and his son Isaac are recorded as lying about their wife being their sister, in order to protect them in a foreign land. Like father, like son?

- What similarity do the stories of Noah and Moses have with each other? The same Hebrew word is used for both the ark that Noah built and the basket that Moses floated in! This Hebrew word is "tebah," and although these vessels were drastically different sizes, they each saved their passengers with God's provision.

- Perhaps reassuringly, Bible heroes were not chosen because they were perfect. Moses at first refused to speak on God's behalf, begging Him to send someone else! He even got his brother Aaron to come along and do much of the talking for him. Jeremiah told God that he was too young to be a prophet. Elijah had a bit of an emotional breakdown after his victory on Mount Carmel, running away to the wilderness out of fear. And of course, Jonah ran so far away from God that he ended up in the belly of a fish!

- In addition to often lacking confidence, Bible heroes were also not immune to sin. Time and time again we see the prophets, military heroes, kings, and even Patriarchs mess up before turning to God again.

There's David and his sin with Bathsheba, Paul and his persecution of Christians, Peter's denial of Christ, and even Noah's unfortunate overconsumption of alcohol after the flood.

- You may not hear his name much today, but one Bible hero is responsible for the division of labor we still use in most business and government systems today! Moses's father-in-law, Jethro, encouraged him to divide his leadership burden between elders that would oversee their portion of each tribe. Moses appointed leaders and sub-leaders over every ten, fifty, one hundred, and one thousand people, freeing up his time to lead and handle only the most important issues.

- Moses's life was divided up into three portions of forty years each. The first forty cover his life in Egypt, the second forty were spent in hiding in the land of Midian, and the final forty cover his role in the Passover and Exodus experience.

- To this day, nobody knows where Moses was buried. The curious reason? Apparently, the angel Michael had to hide his body from Satan who wanted to take charge of it (Jude 1:9). Scripture only says that the Lord Himself "buried him in the valley in the land of Moab opposite Beth-peor (Deuteronomy 34:6)."

CHAPTER 13:
MIRACLES OF JESUS

TRIVIA TIME!

1. How many fish and loaves of bread did Jesus multiply to feed the crowd of 5,000?
   a. Five loaves of bread and two fish
   b. Two loaves of bread and three fish
   c. Ten loaves of bread and ten fish
   d. Two loaves of bread and five fish

2. When Jesus encountered a demon possessed man at the land of Gerasenes, He ordered the evil spirits to:
   a. Leave the man alone
   b. Run away
   c. Go back to Sheol
   d. Go into a herd of swine

3. What was the first miracle of Jesus?
   a. Turning water into wine
   b. Healing the paralytic
   c. Feeding the crowd of 5,000
   d. Casting a demon out of Mary Magdalene

4. Who asked Jesus to turn the water into wine at the wedding at Cana?
    a. Peter
    b. His mother Mary
    c. The host of the wedding
    d. The bride

5. What did Jesus rub on the blind man's eyes?
    a. Medicine
    b. Leaves
    c. Mud
    d. Water

6. Whose mother-in-law did Jesus heal?
    a. John
    b. Peter
    c. Mary
    d. Martha

7. What did Jesus say to Jairus's daughter when he raised her from the dead?
    a. "Little girl, rise!"
    b. "Little girl, take heart!"
    c. "Little girl, eat!"
    d. "Little girl, come here!"

8. What did Jesus's disciples first think when they saw Jesus walking on the water?
    a. He was God
    b. He was a ghost

c. He was a magician
   d. He was an angel

9. Who was the first one to see Jesus after he rose from the dead?
   a. John
   b. Peter
   c. Mary, mother of Jesus
   d. Mary Magdalene

10. True or false: The Bible records all of Jesus's miracles.

11. How did blind Bartimaeus receive his sight?
    a. He cried out to Jesus until He stopped and acknowledged him
    b. He grabbed on to the hem of Jesus's garment as He passed by
    c. He went to the Pool of Siloam to wash in the water
    d. His friends lowered him through the roof where Jesus was speaking

12. Where did Lazarus live when Jesus raised him from the dead?
    a. Bethany
    b. Bethsaida
    c. Bethlehem
    d. Bethphage

13. True or false: Jesus always told people to keep His miracles a secret.

14. How did Jesus respond to the leper who came to Him and said, "Lord, if You are willing, You can make me clean"?

    a. He touched him and said, "I am willing."
    b. He instructed him to go and wash in the Jordan River
    c. He told him to tell everyone
    d. He said that only God could make the man clean

15. In Matthew 17, why were the disciples upset about the demon possessed boy?

    a. They wanted to heal him first but ran out of time
    b. They tried and they could not heal him
    c. They didn't want Jesus to heal him
    d. They felt sorry for his parents

16. In response, Jesus answers them with these famous words:

    a. "This kind does not go out except by prayer and fasting."
    b. "If you have faith like a grain of mustard seed, you will say to this mountain, 'Move from here to there,' and it will move."
    c. "It is not the healthy who need a doctor, but the sick. I have not come to call the righteous, but sinners to repentance."
    d. Both A + B depending on the translation

17. What kind of tree did Jesus curse, causing it to wither up at His words?
    a. A palm tree
    b. A date tree
    c. A fig tree
    d. An olive tree

18. The Pharisees were often upset that Jesus healed ____.
    a. Lepers
    b. On the Sabbath
    c. Gentiles
    d. In the temple

19. True or false: Jesus fed a large crowd with small rations more than once.

20. True or false: Mary Magdalene originally was inhabited by a demon called Legion.

ANSWERS

1. A – Five loaves of bread and two fish (Matthew 14:13-21)
2. D – Go into a herd of swine (Mark 5:1-20)
3. A – Turning water into wine (John 2:11)
4. B – His mother Mary (John 2:3)
5. C – Mud (John 6:9)
6. B – Peter (Luke 4:38-40)
7. A – "Little girl, rise!" (Matthew 9:18-20)
8. B – He was a ghost (Matthew 14:22-23)
9. D – Mary Magdalene (Matthew 28:1)
10. False; John 21:25 says the world could not contain all the books that could be written about the acts of Jesus.
11. A – He cried out to Jesus until He stopped and acknowledged him (Mark 10:46-52)
12. A – Bethany (John 11:38-44)
13. False; Jesus at times told the recipients of His miracles to tell others.
14. A – He touched him and said, "I am willing." (Luke 5:12)

15. B – They tried, and they could not heal him (Matthew 17).

16. D – Both (A) and (B) depending on the translation (Matthew 17:20).

17. C – A fig tree (Mark 11:12-25)

18. B – On the Sabbath

19. True; the Bible records at least two occasions where Jesus fed the multitudes

20. False; Legion was the name given by the host of demons in the man whom Jesus encountered on the far side of Galilee, when he cast them into the pigs (Mark 5:9).

DID YOU KNOW?

- The word "gospel" means "good news" and comes from the Greek word "euangelion." Broken down, the prefix of "eu" carries the meaning of something good, and the word "angelion" means "message" (you can also see where we get the word "angel" from).

- Jesus's ministry as recorded in the four Gospel accounts most likely lasted about three years. This is estimated due to the fact that John's Gospel details three separate annual Passover festivals during his time with Jesus. Many have wondered why His time of ministry was so short, but in that time, He accomplished everything that He was sent to do. It is of note that although we know little about the first thirty years of His life, those decades prepared Jesus for His ministry. Readers who feel they have not yet accomplished what they would like to in life should be encouraged.

- Jesus waited until after the third day to raise his friend Lazarus from the dead because Jews at that time believed that the spirit remained with the body for three days. Waiting until this time had passed was seen as definitively miraculous by those who viewed the miracle of his resurrection.

- Jesus told His followers in John 14:12 that whoever believes in Him "will also do the works that I do; and greater works than these will he do, because I am going to the Father." As confirmation, we see many of the apostles going on to perform healings and miracles of their own throughout the book of Acts.

- Peter, James and John were part of Jesus's innermost circle of followers, specially selected to be able to witness such miracles as the Transfiguration and the raising of Jairus's daughter. They were also present during special intimate times such as during Jesus's night of prayer in the Garden of Gethsemane. Perhaps this special training was for a reason. All three men would go on to take solid positions of leadership and evangelism in the post-resurrection early church.

- In total, scripture records three separate occasions on which Jesus revived someone back from the dead: Jairus's daughter, a widow's son, and his friend Lazarus.

- Three times at key points during Jesus's life and ministry, the audible voice of God spoke in the hearing of the people: at Christ's baptism, transfiguration, and crucifixion.

- Before performing many of His public miracles, Jesus prayed out loud to show the people where His power to perform miracles came from (Acts 2:22). For example: at the feeding of the 5,000 and at the resurrection of Lazarus.

- In a beautiful, intimate moment at the end of John's Gospel, the resurrected Jesus recreates a familiar scene in which he once again instructs Peter, James and John (among others) to let down their nets for a miraculous catch of fish. The moment Peter realizes who is speaking to him, he jumps out of the boat and swims to shore where the disciples enjoy a meal with the Lord.

- Each of the four Gospels records different miracles of Jesus, with some overlap between the books. However, the only miracle recorded in all four accounts is the feeding of the 5,000.

CHAPTER 14:
PARABLES OF JESUS

TRIVIA TIME!

1. Before returning home, the Prodigal Son had resorted to what?

    a. Eating pig slop with the animals he was caring for
    b. Selling himself into slavery
    c. Joining up with an enemy army
    d. Begging for food in the city gate

2. In the parable of the unforgiving servant, what did the servant do to his own debtor after being forgiven of a large debt?

    a. Killed him
    b. Had him thrown in jail
    c. Sold him
    d. Forgave him too

3. In the story of the Good Samaritan, which of the following people passed by a man in need of help on the road?

a. The Samaritan
   b. A Roman soldier
   c. A priest
   d. A group of robbers

4. True or false: In the parable of the talents, the one who spent the money was punished.

5. In the parable of the wheat and the tares, what are the tares?
   a. The righteous
   b. The wicked
   c. Angels
   d. Children

6. Which of these was not an illustration in the parable of the sower?
   a. A path
   b. Rocky soil
   c. Thorns
   d. A vineyard

7. The parable of a woman looking for a lost coin is meant to demonstrate what?
   a. The love of a mother
   b. The value of the Kingdom of God
   c. The persistence of prayer
   d. The joy at one person being saved from death

8. Why did Jesus often use parables in His teaching?

    a. To reveal mysteries to only those willing to understand.
    b. To make His points easier to understand
    c. To conceal the meaning of the parables from His disciples
    d. To hide his works from Satan
9. True or false: There are no parables in the Old Testament.
10. The parable of the lost sheep is about:
    a. A farmer who lost his sheep
    b. The value of one lost person who repents
    c. Ninety-nine sheep are more important than one
    d. What to do when something is missing
11. What does the woman with a lost coin do?
    a. Looks until she finds it
    b. Puts the rest of her coins in the bank for safekeeping
    c. Cries with sorrow
    d. Gives up
12. In the most common interpretation of the parable of the pearl of great price, the pearl represents what?
    a. Life
    b. The Kingdom of Heaven
    c. Great riches and gold
    d. One sinner who repents

13. In the parable of treasure hidden in a field, the field represents what?

    a. Jesus
    b. People
    c. The world
    d. Heaven

14. True or false: Jesus never explained His parables to His disciples.

15. In the parable of the friend at midnight, Jesus says, "Which of you, if your son asks for bread, will give him a ____?"

    a. Scorpion
    b. Fish
    c. Stone
    d. Snake

16. What was the moral of the story of the Good Samaritan?

    a. Be a good neighbor to everyone
    b. Go above and beyond for other people
    c. If you are asked to go one mile, go two miles
    d. The one you least expect will help you

17. The wise man builds his house upon the rock, but the foolish man builds his house upon the ____.

    a. Hill
    b. Mud
    c. Sand
    d. Sea

18. Finish this verse: "If the world hates you, remember that___." (John 15:18)
    a. I have overcome the world
    b. I am with you until the end of the age
    c. It hated Me first
    d. I have chosen you out of the world

19. In the parable of the ten virgins, what did five of the virgins have to go back for?
    a. Lamps
    b. Oil
    c. Coins
    d. A gift

20. True or false: Every parable has only one meaning or explanation.

ANSWERS

1. A – Eating pig slop with the animals he was caring for (Luke 15:11-32)

2. B – Had him thrown in jail (Matthew 18:21-35)

3. C – A priest (Luke 10:30-37)

4. False; the one who buried his talents was punished (Matthew 25:14-30).

5. B – The wicked (Matthew 13:24-30)

6. D – A vineyard (Matthew 13:1-23)

7. D – The joy at one person being saved from death (Luke 15:8-10)

8. A – To reveal mysteries to only those willing to understand

9. False; Ezekiel in particular was instructed to speak in parables (2 Samuel 12:1-14).

10. B – The value of one lost person who repents (Luke 15:1-7)

11. A – Looks until she finds it (Luke 15:8-10)

12. B – The Kingdom of Heaven (Mark 18:45-46)

13. C – The world (Matthew 13:44)

14. False; Jesus often answered his disciples' questions about the parables when they were alone.

15. C – Stone (Matthew 7:9)

16. A – Be a good neighbor to everyone (Luke 10:30-37)

17. C – Sand (Matthew 7:24)

18. C – It hated Me first (John 15:18)

19. B – Oil (Matthew 25:1-12)

20. False; parables often have more than one interpretation, point, or intended meaning.

DID YOU KNOW?

- Jesus did not invent the use of parables. In fact, parables were a common teaching tool of rabbis throughout Jewish history. Many of them are still preserved for us today through the writings of the Talmud. Jesus's Jewish disciples would have been very familiar with this common form of oral literature.

- When Jesus preached His famous words about a child asking his father for bread and that no father would respond by giving a stone, He was actually reversing the story of His temptation in the wilderness. Satan came to Him and said, "If you are the Son of God, command these stones to become loaves of bread." By using the same example in His parable, this story illustrates that our Heavenly Father wants to provide for us.

- We've all heard the story of the Good Samaritan, but why was it so shocking to hear at that time? Just who were the Samaritans? The Samaritans were a group of interracial Jews who had mingled with foreigners from other nations. They had their own temple and their own high priest, rejected the prophets, had their own version of the scriptures, and had tried to stop Nehemiah from rebuilding the city of Jerusalem.

Thus they were seen by the people of Israel as traitors, enemies, unclean, and heretical.

- Jesus's disciples often came to Him privately and asked Him to explain the meaning of His parables. It is important to remember that most of His disciples were probably teenagers at the time that they were called! Therefore, it makes sense they would need frequent, detailed explanations – and that Jesus would be so patient with them.

- John's Gospel curiously contains no parables. On the other hand, the synoptic Gospels record several dozen unique parables of Jesus in total. The Gospel of Luke records the most.

- The most famous of Jesus's parables are: The Good Samaritan and the Prodigal Son.

- Many of Jesus's parables may have been delivered at a spot known today as "The Bay of Parables," a little cove situated halfway between Capernaum and Tabgha where the natural acoustics would have made a perfect teaching spot.

- As Jesus was teaching, His parables often included many details that would have been visible right there in the landscape around Him. For example, the different types of ground in the Parable of the Sower or the yellow mustard plant from the Parable of the Mustard Seed.

- Jesus often grouped His parables thematically, giving two or three examples of the same topic to help illustrate His point.
- There are two additional parables found in the non-canonical book of possible sayings of Jesus known as the "Gospel of Thomas." They include the Parable of the Assassin and the Parable of the Empty Jar.
- Many of the parables detailed in Matthew, Luke, and Mark may have originally come from a document known as the Q document, which has yet to be found.

CHAPTER 15:
BIBLICAL HISTORY & ARCHEOLOGY

TRIVIA TIME!

1. This collection of ancient documents was discovered when a young shepherd boy threw a rock into a cave:
    a. The Aramaic Targums
    b. The Masoretic Text
    c. The Dead Sea Scrolls
    d. The Aleppo Codex

2. Why did the Northern Kingdom of Israel split off from the Southern Kingdom?
    a. Because King Solomon began to rebel against God
    b. Because there wasn't enough room in the land of Judah
    c. Because they wanted to make their own temple in Nazareth
    d. Because they didn't like King David

3. This King sent out a decree allowing for the Israelites to go back and rebuild the second temple:
    a. King Xerxes
    b. King Cyrus
    c. King Ahasuerus
    d. King Sennacherib

4. The Ark of the Covenant contained all of the following except:
    a. Aaron's budding staff
    b. A jar of Manna
    c. The 10 Commandments
    d. A golden ephod

5. Which of these was not the name of a Jerusalem gate in ancient times?
    a. The Lion Gate
    b. The Sheep Gate
    c. The Dung Gate
    d. The Fish Gate

6. True or false: Archeological evidence of Roman crucifixion has been found.

7. Which of these was not originally used as a symbol for the early church?
    a. The fish
    b. The anchor
    c. The cross
    d. The dove

8. This early "church father" was said to be a direct disciple of the Apostle John:
    a. Polycarp
    b. Tertullian
    c. Justin Martyr
    d. Irenaeus

9. What important event occurred at Hebron?
    a. The battle of the Amalekites
    b. The burial of Abraham and Sarah
    c. David and Goliath
    d. The anointing of King Saul

10. All of the following sites can still be visited today except:
    a. The field where David slew Goliath
    b. The Cave of the Patriarchs
    c. The Gihon Spring where kings were anointed
    d. Joseph's jail cell in Egypt

11. In addition to Greek and Hebrew, some parts of the Bible were written in this language:
    a. Latin
    b. Aramaic
    c. Arabic
    d. English

12. Who was the High Priest at the time of Jesus's death?
    a. Pontius Pilate
    b. Herod

c. Caiaphas
d. Nicodemus

13. True or false: There is no archeological evidence to prove the First Temple Period.

14. Archeological evidence supports which fact about ancient Jericho:
    a. The walls had fallen outward
    b. The Israelites had marched around it with trumpets
    c. There was a man named Joshua who conquered it
    d. The city was under siege for exactly 7 days

15. This Biblical city is purported to be one of the oldest in the world:
    a. Jericho
    b. Jerusalem
    c. Ai
    d. Babylon

16. Visitors to Jerusalem today can still visit which of these sites:
    a. A trail of ancient Jewish purity baths leading up to the temple
    b. The pool of Siloam where a blind man was healed by Jesus
    c. An underground tunnel that was built by King Hezekiah
    d. All of the above

17. The Dead Sea Scrolls were found in:
    a. Jerusalem
    b. Qumran
    c. Jericho
    d. Eliat

18. Visitors to the Galilee region of Israel today can still visit all of these sites EXCEPT:
    a. An ancient synagogue where Jesus likely taught
    b. The house of Peter's family
    c. The house of Jesus's family
    d. The beach where Jesus ate with His disciples after His resurrection

19. True or false: The Ark of the Covenant has been found and is on display in an Israeli museum today.

20. True or false: Many ancient societies around the world have a similar story in their culture about a massive flood.

ANSWERS

1. C – Dead Sea Scrolls
2. A – Because King Solomon began to rebel against God (1 Kings 12:19)
3. B – King Cyrus (Ezra 1:1-6:22)
4. D – A golden ephod (Hebrews 9:3-4)
5. A – The Lion Gate
6. True; in addition to written records, physical evidence of bones was found.
7. C – The cross
8. A – Polycarp
9. B – The burial of Abraham and Sarah
10. D – Joseph's jail cell in Egypt
11. B – Aramaic
12. C – Caiaphas (John 22:51)
13. False; there is ample evidence from this time period, including many seal stamps like a recent discovery found bearing the name of Nathan-Melech (2 Kings 23:11).
14. A – The walls fell outward
15. A – Jericho

16. D – All of the above

17. B – Qumran

18. C – The house of Jesus's family

19. False; the fate of the Ark of the Covenant is one of the biggest historical and archeological mysteries to date.

20. True; almost every ancient civilization has some variation of a flood story.

DID YOU KNOW?

- The Old Testament, which is written in Hebrew, would have been read from right to left instead of from left to right. Hebrew books are also opened from the opposite cover than most books in English that you would see today.

- The shortest book in the Old Testament is Obadiah, with just 440 words in the original language it was written in (Hebrew).

- The shortest book in the entire Bible is the letter known as 3 John, which contains just 219 words in its original language. 2 John is a close second with just 245 words in the original language.

- The word "Bible" itself simply means "book" or "scroll." And in the days that they were first written, the scriptures were housed in individual scrolls that must be unrolled in order to be read. In those days, because many people did not know how to read or write, they would have heard the words of the Bible read out loud instead of reading it for themselves. We see evidence of this in Luke 4 when Jesus reads from the scroll of Isaiah in the synagogue at Nazareth.

- The Bible originally did not have chapters or verses. The scripture divisions you see today were added during the production of more modern translations starting around the 1500s.

- When Jesus referred to "jots and tittles" in Matthew 5:18, He was referring to the smallest letter of the Hebrew alphabet (a jot) and a small extending line added to some Hebrew letters (a tittle). For thousands of years, Israelite scribes were meticulous about copying the scriptures word for word, jot for jot. They had to be careful and pay great attention to detail because the smallest error could make a big difference in the meaning between two words.

- Many of the names you see in your Bible today are not the original Hebrew and Greek names your favorite characters were actually called. For example, did you know that Mary's name was actually Miriam and Jesus's name was most likely Yeshua? At the time of Jesus's birth, there was no letter J in the Hebrew alphabet.

- In addition, nearly every name in the Bible has an important meaning. For example, Jesus's name "Yeshua" means "God's salvation," Daniel means "God is my judge," and Noah means "rest." Oftentimes, these names can give us a clue as to what God was doing through mankind in His redemptive story.

- According to Jewish tradition, the date of destruction for both temples was the 9th of Av, a day of mourning and fasting still observed today, known as Tisha B'Av.

- The construction of the first temple under King Solomon took about a decade to complete and more than 150,000 workers! The second temple took about 2 decades to complete, with many delays and pauses to the work.

- If you were a visitor to the temple, you would have seen different courts for men, women, and Gentiles. Archeological evidence points to the fact that there were posted warnings for anyone who would enter beyond the court of the Gentiles. In addition, the high priest was the only one who could enter the Holy of Holies.

- There is a life-size (almost) to scale model of the first Jewish temple in São Paulo, Brazil. The project took more than $300 million to create. Visitors today can enter, pray, attend worship services and even Sunday School classes.

- There are more copies of the New Testament in existence today than any other ancient document, with more than 25,000 complete or fragmented manuscripts remaining, and in several languages. In addition, there are so many quotations of the New Testament scriptures in the writings of the "church fathers" that a complete copy could be reconstructed from their quotes alone!

- Jesus's famous words to Peter in Matthew 16 about the gates of hell not prevailing against the church were most likely spoken because they were at Caesarea Philippi, which was a center of Pagan worship near Mount Hermon. Tradition is that this site may have been known as "the gates of hades" or hell.

- The number forty is often associated with a period of testing in the Bible. Some examples include the forty days and forty nights that rain flooded the earth while Noah was in the ark and the forty days and forty nights that Jesus was tempted in the wilderness. In addition, the Israelites were in the desert wandering for 40 years after the first generation to leave Egypt failed God's tests to be faithful to Him.

- Archeological discoveries have found that the use of "tear bottles" was widespread among many ancient cultures, including Jewish, Roman, and Greek societies. It is difficult to tell if this custom proceeded the writing of Psalm 56:8 ("You have kept count of my tossings; put my tears in your bottle. Are they not in your book?") or it was a result of it. But this beautiful custom also brings to mind Revelation 21:4 ("He will wipe away every tear from their eyes, and death shall be no more, neither shall there be mourning, nor crying, nor pain anymore, for the former things have passed away.")

www.ingramcontent.com/pod-product-compliance
Lightning Source LLC
Chambersburg PA
CBHW071450070526
44578CB00001B/291